MISTER OWITA'S
Guide to
GARDENING

MISTER OWITA'S

Guide to

GARDENING

HOW I LEARNED THE UNEXPECTED
JOY OF A GREEN THUMB AND
AN OPEN HEART

CAROL WALL

AMY EINHORN BOOKS
Published by G. P. Putnam's Sons
a member of
Penguin Group (USA)
New York

AMY EINHORN BOOKS
Published by G. P. Putnam's Sons
Publishers Since 1838
Published by the Penguin Group
Penguin Group (USA) LLC
375 Hudson Street
New York, New York 10014

USA · Canada · UK · Ireland · Australia
New Zealand · India · South Africa · China

penguin.com
A Penguin Random House Company

Library of Congress Cataloging-in-Publication Data

Wall, Carol, date.
Mister Owita's guide to gardening : how I learned the unexpected joy
of a green thumb and an open heart / Carol Wall.
p.   cm.
ISBN 978-0-399-15798-1
1. Gardening—Philosophy.   2. Intercultural communication.   I. Title.
SB454.3.P45W35   2014   2013036314
635—dc23

Printed in the United States of America
1   3   5   7   9   10   8   6   4   2

BOOK DESIGN BY MICHELLE MCMILLIAN

Contents

To my husband, Dick

Prologue

I never liked getting my hands dirty. This was one reason that our yard looked so sad. But there were other reasons, too—bigger reasons that were much harder to confront than brittle grass and overgrown bushes.

It's not that I was ignoring our yard on purpose. Every once in a while we hired someone to plant or trim something. My husband, Dick, did his share of mowing. But he never did it happily. We weren't yard-proud the way some people are. And when the kids were young, there was always something more important than yard work to do. Going to one of their games or events, running them to school and lessons, or shepherding them to doctor appointments—all those things ranked way higher on our list of priorities.

Once the kids were grown, I still managed to find more important things to do. I much preferred reading a book, or watching a documentary on TV, or going out to dinner with Dick to pruning a bush. I loved our house, and I enjoyed decorating the inside, but there was never anything about *maintaining* a house that I enjoyed. In some couples, one spouse makes up for the flaws of the other. But for better or worse, my beloved spouse and I shared the same flaw in this department. Neither of us was handy. We ignored our loose front doorknob until it went from shaky to wobbly and finally fell off when we tried to exit the house one evening. Dick watched it fall to the hardwood floor with a thunk, then looked at me and said, "Time to move."

I don't think we were entirely wrong in holding on to our low-intervention policy. Once when Dick and I were walking through town, we were stopped by a group of young women who were celebrating their friend's upcoming wedding. They were asking all the obviously married women they saw for advice for the new bride. I said, "You know, my life really began when I got married." They all laughed and told me that I was the first woman they'd stopped who hadn't said, "Don't do it." Then I told them that my best advice was not to approach marriage like it was an arrangement between property co-owners. It seemed to me like too many people spent too much of their time taking care of their houses instead of enjoying their spouses. And where was the fun in that?

I liked to think that it was a valid philosophy of life that kept me out of the yard, and not just sheer laziness. In any case, to me, even worse than digging out a screwdriver to fix our door-knob would have been digging in the dirt. I had zero interest in that area of our property. I don't think I even really looked at it.

Then one day, I noticed that our yard had slowly, gradually transformed itself. No longer could I flatter myself that it was natural and unmanicured because that was the aesthetic I pre-ferred. No, our yard wasn't just rough around the edges. It had become a genuine embarrassment. Maybe we didn't have the worst yard on the block. But we were close to it, and one good mowing in our most neglectful neighbor's yard might easily nudge us into the bottom slot. And that just wouldn't do. I might never have been yard-proud, but I did not want to be yard-ashamed.

So I decided that it was time to do something about this situation. It was a fixable problem, after all—and how nice it was to have one of those.

When I passed our neighbor Sarah's yard I couldn't help see-ing what an amazing job her gardener had done. Sarah was a master gardener herself, but recently she'd gotten busy at work and had brought in some help. And even I could tell that a true artist was at work there. Maybe I could hire her gardener, I thought to myself. And then our yard would be as beautiful as hers. It would be healthy and lush and well taken care of—just the way I wanted to be myself.

A few days later I saw the mystery gardener in the flesh—the artist who'd wrought such a miracle transformation in my neigh-bor's yard—and it was kismet. Love at first sight. No, it wasn't the kind of love that causes you to question your marriage. It was the kind of love that causes you to question yourself. The kind that makes you want to be a better person. The kind that changes your life completely.

His name was Giles Owita, and from the start, something flowered between us and around us. First he became my gardener, and then he became my friend. And while I knew from the moment I met him that he was someone special—truly, I didn't know the half of it.

I.

Garden Angel

The well-tended yard and stately home of my neighbor Sarah Driscoll, Master Gardener, slipped by on my right. I was so arrested by the view that, for an instant, it felt as if I were standing still and her forty-foot magnolia tree were moving backward.

Then I saw him.

He wore a navy work suit with bright white leather tennis shoes. Our eyes met briefly and my foot went to the brake. Just as fast as that.

By then he'd already turned away from me. I watched as he plunged his shovel into a mound of mulch that wasn't there when I had left home that morning. He gingerly eased the shovel out and balanced a small pyramid of shredded hardwood with what appeared to be a practiced hand. His build was slight and strong.

I knew that Sarah's new gardener also worked with her at the Garden Shoppe, where she was assistant manager. She'd said he was industrious and talented. As I continued down the hill and pulled into my driveway, I followed his reflection in my rearview mirror. I kept watching as he moved toward Sarah's boxwoods, where he let the mulch slide from his shovel into empty portions of the newly cut bed. He glanced down the hill, in my direction, as if curious himself. Or else he was wondering why that lady with the unfortunate yard was staring at him. That caught me up short. I didn't want to be the white lady staring at the black stranger in the neighborhood. I'd encountered too many small-minded people like that over the years, and I had a horror of seeming like one of them.

It was the second week of March, just after five o'clock, and I was fifty-two years old. Even now I can imagine recording those details in a mental journal, as if I already knew that this moment—the first time I laid eyes on Giles Owita—was something I'd always remember. It was within that sliver of awareness that I noticed the newly sprouting lime-green grass in Sarah's yard, and the fresh leaves on the maple trees that lined our neighborhood's sidewalk. Some overhanging branches, not yet full and leafy-green, curved in almost perfect symmetry above the stranger's head, and I was reminded of an abstract and imperfect halo. Everything about this man, from the lush green of the plants he worked on to the coiled energy that seemed to direct his movements, exuded health. I envied him this blessing.

Almost ten years had passed since I was first diagnosed with cancer in my left breast, but I still felt shaken. Not that anyone other than my husband knew this. If you were a friend of mine in those days, you would have said, *She handled it so well, both the lumpectomy and the radiation. She went right on with her activities and didn't complain. Her faith was strengthened. She was not afraid. She was a wonderful example for all of us.* But none of this would have been true. Secretly, I was an utter coward. I felt marked—doomed. I had been heartsick and consumed by fear. I worried then, and I have worried every day since then. I had spent too many hours in the past ten years examining my body for bad omens.

The sky was tinged with the lovely light blues and pinks of late afternoon. I parked in our driveway and walked toward our brick front porch, all the while thinking of luck and prayers— the ones that seemed to get answered and the ones that didn't. Upstairs in my bedroom, tucked away in my jewelry box, I still had a little prayer in the form of a poem I wrote for my children before my surgery almost ten years ago. That prayer had worked—I'd lived to see all three of them grown up, and I hoped to live a lot longer yet. But hope was a fragile thing, and if that poem symbolized an answered prayer for me, it also reminded me that our hold on everything we love is tenuous. The more we cherish, the more we fear losing.

I twisted my front-door key to the sounds of our beagle, Rhudy, scrambling through the foyer. I let him out through the screen door and into the backyard. A few minutes later, with my glass of sweet iced tea, I stood at our kitchen window, gazing at the creek. The waters tumbled fast with the season's thaw. Rhudy sniffed along the fence line. Shadows of trees shifted and mingled with each other on the green-painted asphalt of the basketball court where our children used to play. With creeping embarrassment I noticed the following: muddy splotches in the midst of thinning grass, shrubbery turned brown or wild and out of control, the whole yard littered with twigs blown by the wind, horrifying whorls of crabgrass. It looked shabby. And this was what our neighbors had as their view every day.

I ventured back outside again and up the hill, my footsteps falling at a steady pace on the concrete sidewalk. I walked through Sarah's front yard and peered over the fence into the back. I saw no trace of the stranger. I pulled my cell phone from my jacket pocket and called Sarah's number. It went straight to voice mail so I left her a message: "Hey—it's Carol. I saw the new guy working in your yard. Do you think he's got time for another client?"

I lingered at the fence and looked at Sarah's meditation garden. Last year, she had added a charming pebble path that wound its way through a tumble of gardenias and calla lilies. There were wrought-iron benches, and an especially lovely garden angel cast in concrete served as a focal point. My world was about to expand in unexpected ways, but all I noticed on that cloudless day was a yard that made me feel inferior. Envy, thy name is Carol Wall.

I walked back down the hill to my house. Rhudy barked from the backyard, but I just kept going indoors. Fatigue caught up with me. Not for the first time, I wondered why it was that some people could bounce from work to the grocery store and back home again, and then immediately make a smiling, nourishing meal for all their family to enjoy. That's never been me. We'd had plenty of lovely meals together as a family, and our home had been filled with joy. But whenever I walked in the door after a long day at work the first thing I looked for was a chair. I needed to recharge my batteries. Then, after a half hour or so I could get up again.

When we moved from Radford to Roanoke and all the painting and decorating was complete, I looked at my three children and I said, "Go upstairs, take Rhudy with you, and don't come down again until you're grown." Of course I was joking (sort of). Our lives were a jumble of dueling schedules—teaching high school for me, practicing law for my husband, plus all the children's practices for sports, dance and piano lessons, and recitals. Not to mention the emergencies that multiplied with each child you brought into the world. The chaos grounded me in daily things that had to be done for others. There was our older son Chad's learning disability that he bravely overcame, our daughter Jennie's terrifying brush with melanoma (a growth that turned out to be benign, but not before scaring the living daylights out of all of us), and our younger son Phil's nearly devastating loss of a functioning thyroid. As a result he'd tumbled into a deep depression at just eleven years old—the very same year that I received my cancer diagnosis. That was not a good year.

With my son's illness to occupy my thoughts, there was little time left to worry about myself, but I managed to pencil it in anyway. Would the cancer come back? That was a question I'd asked every day of my life, sometimes multiple times. The odds were stacked heavily against recurrence. At least that is what I was told by my Handsome Oncologist (I named him this without fear of contradiction). But when the "C" word has been mentioned even once in your life, the diagnosis is a ghost that chases you forever after. It's best to keep moving, as fast as possible. If, now and then, I paused in front of a mirror, it was only to rearrange my bangs or freshen up my lipstick. I dared not look too closely, for fear of finding a lump, bump, mole, or other symptom someone had missed. This had become my life.

I'd always thought of myself as the caregiver—the one whose lot in life was to *bring* the casserole and not to receive it. Way back in seventh grade when we were giving student government speeches, I noticed a friend of mine was about to faint right in the middle of her address. I got up without hesitating, went to her, and said, "Patty, you need to sit down." I still recall how deeply satisfying it was to me that I was able to help. I thought to myself even then, *That's the kind of person I am. I keep my poise under fire, and I help those who are in need.* But breast cancer flipped my whole sense of self on its head. I had the oddest sensation that God had gotten me mixed up with someone else.

Perhaps that was why my friends all thought I'd triumphed so beautifully over my cancer diagnosis. I found my illness so shameful, so embarrassing, that I simply refused to confide in anyone other than Dick about my fears. I also disliked the way that cancer exposed me. An introvert by nature, I found it unsettling how people felt completely comfortable asking for the most intimate details about my illness and treatment. Bless their hearts, I knew that when friends called me, they'd already done their research—they would have asked someone else how my most recent test results had turned out, so they'd know whether the news was good or bad. I felt like I was walking around town with a big "C" for cancer emblazoned on my chest. In our smallish town, the quest for fresh gossip could be intense. It was a kind of currency that people exchanged. And I hated the feeling that my illness had become fodder for talk, well intentioned or not.

I also didn't feel like I could be as positive as everyone expected me to be. I didn't want to wear pink, or claim I felt bright and rosy about the future, when in truth I was often terrified. I had learned the hard way that people don't want to hear that kind of talk from cancer survivors—it sounds so defeatist to their ears. But I figured I was entitled to feel a little discouraged. Cancer made me realize that I was not in charge of things, and I never was. That scared me, and it downright terrified Dick. He hated it when I sounded negative. He wanted us to focus on the upside. He constantly reminded me that the doctors had said the cancer was unlikely to come back—I just needed to be careful, to remain vigilant, and to withstand the agonizing wait for test results after every mammogram. That was easy for him to say.

So I pushed down my fears. But like the situation in our yard, the more I tried to ignore them, the more my fears grew and blossomed into anger. They turned wild and uncontrollable, their roots tripping me up when I least expected it. I wished there was a gardener who could help me with that particular problem. Instead, I'd settle for some improvement in the crabgrass, and the help of the stranger who'd worked such miracles in my neighbor's yard.

PRAYER FOR MY CHILDREN, AGES 16, 13, AND 10

[Written with Trembling Hand, on the Eve of the Biopsy that Followed a "Suspicious" Mammogram]

May nothing bad ever happen to them, Dear Lord
May they look to the top of the hill
and see me walking toward them, through the meadow
May they never fear abandonment of any kind
May I be well
May I be there
For I'm their Mother.
Amen.

2.

Of Particular Beauty
Are the Azaleas

Heavy drops of rain stung my face and peppered my hair as I hurried down the sidewalk toward my front door. I flipped up the hood of my khaki raincoat and lowered my head against the onslaught, which now included pellets of hail. In my rush to get inside, I almost missed the folded piece of paper dangling from the antiquated letter slot that sat low and to the right of our front door.

The paper trembled in the wind like something delicate, alive. I grasped it, guessing it to be some sort of flyer. Maybe an ad for pizza, or perhaps a two-for-one deal at the new Chinese buffet in the strip mall where we bought our groceries. With little thought, I slipped it under my thumb, holding it against the book I was carrying. Inside, I unfolded the mystery page enough to see the general features of a handwritten letter. Dampness had obscured some lines of writing at the top, where the date should have been, but the rest was dry.

Rhudy put his paws high up on my legs and stretched mightily, as if sleeping in his favorite chair for hours had been exhausting. He trotted into the kitchen and sat by the refrigerator for his treat, but I made him wait. Curious now, I went to the dining room table and smoothed the letter open.

It was written in pen and began with a proper salutation, "Dear Mrs. Wall." The handwriting was distinctive, with narrow letters listing to the right, as if a breeze were trying to blow them off the page. The signature at the bottom, "Giles Owita," was composed of letters slightly larger than the text of the letter itself. He had written his phone number below his signature.

Dear Mrs. Wall,

Mrs. Driscoll has given me your message. Thank you very much. I took the liberty of stopping by your compound today, even though your vehicle was not in the driveway. Your little beagle peered out at me with happy barks of warning from his window by the door. You are fortunate to have his services. You have a very beautiful yard, with many well-established specimens. Certain plants will benefit from pruning. We might even say they are over-flourishing. Of particular beauty are the azaleas. We will prune them just as soon as they have bloomed, being careful to complete the process before they have set their buds for next year. In the meantime, we can apply certain chemicals, which I am only too happy to furnish, as some remain from another project I undertook across town. We will discuss the further plan when next we meet, but for now, I am delighted to accept the job at your compound. I must go on to another assignment for the evening, but will look forward to meeting you soon.

Erokamano,

(This means "thank you," in Luo, my mother tongue)

Giles Owita

I stared out the window.

Erokamano.

Could I possibly remember this?

I would like to, just to make him feel at home.

The wind pushed holly branches thick with thorny leaves against the panes of the window. They made a stubborn screeching sound. Heavy drops of hail pecked the glass and caused the glossy leaves to tremble. I sighed, because this particular holly plant, the favorite of a former owner of the house from the 1950s (I'd been told), had been overgrown for years. Holly is a bush that's more like a tree and grows with a vengeance, especially when cut to the root, a procedure Dick and I had attempted only once, because of the nasty thorns. How would this Giles Owita react to being asked to do a thankless task like that? Would he be up to it? Or even know where to begin? I recalled his look of quiet dignity as he stood by the mulch pile in Sarah's driveway. He would certainly try to prune the holly, I concluded. He looked conscientious, and would do his best to please.

I wasn't sure why this note from a stranger had so captured my fancy. Maybe it was my English teacher gene. The letter was longer than it needed to be, and there was a kind of poetry to it. I was enchanted that he'd thought to write at all, that he hadn't settled for a quick phone conversation, the way most people would have. Then I wondered, *Why* did *he take the trouble to pen a note, instead of calling me?* Sarah had told me he was from Kenya originally, and clearly English was his second language. Perhaps he had a heavy accent that made him feel awkward in spoken conversation. If only he knew I once taught English as a second language, maybe he wouldn't be so nervous. It had been quite a few years since I taught the ESL classes, but how well I remembered the struggles and triumphs of my earnest students from other regions of our whirling planet.

I jotted the Luo word for "thank you" in the margin of my notepad I routinely kept by my side (as a teacher I've found they're a necessity), in case I had occasion to express my thanks to Giles Owita. Sitting at the oval table, I began to daydream—one of my very favorite activities. The wind died down. The rain continued, but was gentler as its tiny droplets tapped the leaves. The antique brick of my neighbor's house created a pleasing backdrop for the holly.

The man who wrote my note seemed cheerful (the word "happy" appeared twice, and in the next-to-last sentence, he was "delighted," he said). He did, in fact, seem like the kind of person who might take up a thorny project without complaint. I thought how our neighbors deserved to be rewarded with some pleasant views through their dining room windows, for a change. All that my yard needed was the right person to come along and rid it of imperfections. In an irrational leap of fancy I thought that if that green space outside my window could be made beautiful, then maybe I could return to having hopes for a life where anything associated with me would effortlessly flourish, bloom, delight, and favorably impress.

There was just one teensy problem—a fly in the ointment of my fantasy. There was a line in Giles Owita's letter that gave me pause.

Of particular beauty are the azaleas.

I read it again, and then looked up, envisioning a scene in which I explained to Giles Owita—in my softest, gentlest tone of voice—that I detested azaleas and wanted all three bushes removed. Also put there by the former owner, the azalea bushes lined up on the downward slope at the left side of our house, and I'd always hated them. I found their competing hues suggestive of miniature golf courses where windmills sliced through beds of multicolored tulips. Or theme parks with gaudy clumps of plantings—the kind of rip-off places where my children used to complain of motion sickness and beg for tacky souvenirs.

I wondered how Giles Owita would react to such an essential disagreement over the aesthetic appeal of azaleas. I told myself that I couldn't possibly be the first person to dislike something he loved. In any case, my mind was made up. Giles Owita might balk, but something told me that his better nature and impeccable manners would lead him to comply. Not to mention, it was my yard and he would be working for me. That was something I wouldn't say aloud, because I wouldn't have to. We'd both be well aware of our relative positions in the matter.

Still, I hated to be disagreeable. So I thought of a compromise. To help the pill go down easier, I'd let Giles Owita help me select what to plant in place of the azaleas. That would smooth any ruffled feathers. I could even visit him at his job at the Garden Shoppe, where I could make a big show of loudly touting his skills, his strength in tugging things out of the ground, his knowledge of fertilizers, and so on. I'd praise Giles Owita in a way that would impress Sarah and her boss, Melanie.

Rhudy gave a little whisper-bark. It was a reminder about his promised treat, and probably not the first one he'd given me while I was busy planning. Giles Owita's note described our little beagle with such warmth and humor. That part of the letter made me feel as if I'd somehow known Giles Owita before, though of course, that wasn't possible.

My eyes passed over the sentence: *You are fortunate to have his services.* I glanced at Rhudy. Funny, but I'd never framed it for myself this way—that being a dog was Rhudy's job. After Phil, our youngest, had been diagnosed with his thyroid problem and found himself exhausted and lonely, he begged us for a dog, something we swore we'd never have. But we couldn't say no to Phil, not after everything he'd been through. I still remembered that year's Saint Francis Mass at the Catholic school where I taught. The younger children all brought their pets to the altar for a blessing from the priest. There were puppies on red or purple nylon leashes, cats peering over children's shoulders, parrots carried in cages, and even beloved goldfish circling in bowls. The year we brought Rhudy into our lives, Phil was one of those children walking up to the altar. Rhudy easily fit in the palms of Phil's little hands. When he lifted his puppy toward the priest, I remembered the words of Genesis, in which God declares that everything He made is "Good." Rhudy was certainly one of God's blessed creatures, and a deep gratitude grew in our hearts as, day by day, the lively puppy joined Phil for his frequent naps. Eventually, Phil's health was restored. Giles Owita was certainly right about Rhudy—we were fortunate to have his services.

In the kitchen, I tossed Rhudy a treat. He deftly snagged it in midair.

Giles Owita.

Just the name was intriguing.

Compound.

It sounded elegant, exotic.

Giles Owita seemed inclined to elevate and honor everyone and everything. I told myself that I would call him tomorrow and thank him for leaving such a lovely note.

Erokamano. (I remembered.)

3.

A Rose Between Two Thorns

I became single-mindedly focused on my mission to transform our yard. I had barely finished mulling over Giles Owita's letter before I decided to compile a list of my own to prepare for his visit the following week. I grabbed my grocery pad and set my pen against the narrow page:

1. Please remove azaleas.
2. That holly on the driveway side . . . trim a little?
   (& watch for thorns)
3. Help with our grass!

I scribbled away, adding more projects and ideas, some with question marks. What to plant in place of the azaleas? More box-woods? No, we had too many of those already.

The phone rang and it was Dick. I knew I should have been listening attentively to details about his business trip that had taken him out of town until midweek. Instead, as he explained the dilemmas of his clients, a well-heeled couple with a second home at the beach, my mind drifted. Maybe rhododendrons to replace the azaleas? Sarah told me that sometimes even our local supermarket, Foodland, sold rhododendrons. We needed groceries anyway, so I decided to drive over and take a look.

The temperature had dipped into the upper forties and a steady drizzle kept my windshield wipers busy. The wheels of my van made sounds like paper crinkling on the rain-slick pavement. As I stepped out of the van in the Foodland parking lot, my red umbrella bloomed like a giant flower above my head. I raced against the slant of droplets falling at an angle. My eye took in some random potted plants, but I didn't see rhododendrons. Oh, well. We still needed groceries.

I yanked a cart from the stack. In the produce section, fluorescent lights made a buzzing sound. I inspected a Red Delicious apple, idly turning it over in my hand before changing my mind and letting it roll from my fingertips, back into the bin. Farther down the row, I paused again, examining a head of organic lettuce. It was small, but supple and richly green. I slid it into a plastic bag and put it in my cart.

I lifted my eyes to the aisle markers overhead, pondering where to turn next, when I noticed a familiar-looking figure working at a distance.

Was it . . . Giles Owita?

No. Absolutely not. He couldn't work at Foodland, bagging groceries. He worked at the Garden Shoppe. And he worked in people's yards. How could he have the time to work here as well?

Yet the face was unmistakable. And he gave off a distinctive energy, as if he idled at a higher speed than everybody else. I'd found the author of my charming, hand-delivered note, but he wasn't sitting at a desk waxing poetic or even tending flowers in a garden. Instead, engaged in conversation with a customer, he lowered celery hearts into a paper bag with care, as if it were the most delightful and important job in the world.

I noticed a carousel rack holding gift cards just a few feet away from the line where Giles Owita was bagging groceries. I pretended to be engrossed in browsing and was careful to keep the rack between me and the register. There could be no sane argument for why I felt the need to spy on him, and yet for some reason I was compelled. Giles Owita looked to be about my age, around fifty. He wore khaki pants, a white knit shirt, and his navy Foodland apron tied at the waist. He leaned over the counter, snagging groceries from the rolling belt, comfortable even when he stood off-balance. He seemed to like making things easier for others. As I watched, he grasped a can of soup that rolled beyond the cashier. He deftly scooped up a receipt that slipped from a customer's grasp to the polished floor. His hands performed repetitive tasks, but he never seemed bored or resentful. He seemed like a man who'd already found the peace that everyone on God's green earth was searching for.

Something else struck me as I watched him work. He seemed more comfortable, more at ease than when I'd seen him working in Sarah's yard. Was it because he knew that I was watching him then? I wondered again what he'd thought of the white neighbor lady hitting the brakes. Did he feel threatened when I slowed so abruptly, just enough to stare at him, but not to raise a hand in greeting? Was my creeping vehicle suggestive of neighborly disapproval?

I should have stopped the van, gotten out, and introduced myself. Then, we might have exchanged the brief "hello" that changed everything between two people. How could I have gotten such a simple thing so wrong? *Oh, Lord,* I prayed. *It's me again—Carol. Please help me to be the kind of person my parents raised.* I'd always prided myself on being hypersensitive to racial insult and misunderstanding. I so hoped that I hadn't been guilty of making Giles Owita uncomfortable. My parents would have been utterly disgusted with me if I had—that was not what a "quality person" did, my mother would have said. A quality person knew that we were all the same under the skin.

When I was five years old, in the summer of 1956, my parents, younger sister, and I traveled to Mississippi to visit our cousins who lived in Pascagoula, on the Gulf Coast. It was the first time in my life that I had been faced with segregated bathrooms and water fountains, and at the age of five I had no idea what I was seeing. The farther south we traveled from our home in southwest Virginia, the more we noticed the strange signs. How well I remembered my mother looking down at the sidewalk when I asked what the signs on the two identical water fountains meant. The silence was heavy as we stood before those fountains, all of us hot and thirsty in the days before air-conditioning. There was no way for me to know what could cause my mother's lovely eyes with their long lashes to look so sad. There was something she didn't want to tell me. It was an odd sensation, because in normal circumstances, she was always eager to explain the world to us. I couldn't read yet, but it was perfectly obvious that the letters on the placards ("Colored" and "White") were there for a reason. I don't recall the words my mother spoke, but I do recall the weary regret in her voice and the way she held our hands protectively as we stole a drink, or so it seemed, from one of the fountains. She, on the other hand, couldn't bring herself to take a sip.

My parents were of one mind about this. Daddy ran a small hotel, and he had caused a stir in our hometown of Radford by renting a room to a "Negro." My mother, an only child who grew up during the Depression, had decided that the home she built with Daddy would, first of all, be rich in wisdom and in loving kindness. No one would ever be excluded from her universe or ours. We were as good as anyone, we were taught, but better than no one. Daddy would sometimes quote from FDR's fourth inaugural speech, about being "citizens of the world," and added, in a warning tone, that a child of his would be *that*, and not "an ignoramus or a country bumpkin who looks down on other people."

Examining my conscience, still hiding behind the greeting

cards, I made a decision. With my eyes on Giles Owita, I rolled my cart to take a place in his line. I would do now what I hadn't done before. I would introduce myself the proper way.

Several people were ahead of me in line, and closer in now, I heard their conversations. Giles Owita glanced up in my direction, but if he recognized me, he didn't show it. He continued being cheerful as he lifted groceries from the conveyor belt, somehow managing to train his attention on people instead of the things rolling by him. His eyes were dark, I noticed, but somehow bright as well. His goodwill seemed infectious. He spoke a few words here and there, such as: "Let me reach that for you," or "Our grass is thirsty for this rain. Eh?" He had a lovely, lyrical accent, and I noted how other shoppers actually seemed reluctant to turn away from him to take their groceries home.

I realized that one of them, a younger woman with a baby, was a neighbor of ours whom I hadn't recognized at first. She always seemed to me to wear a permanently sour expression. But today she exchanged pleasantries with Giles Owita as she pushed the curls of her dark brown hair away from her pretty face. Her baby's fingers reached to touch her lips. She kissed the baby's cheek and he rocked in her arms with delight.

I turned in time to see a young man approach the line, carrying a cone of green tissue paper containing roses mingled with baby's breath. He was newly married, I decided. Or recently engaged. Maybe his wife had just had a baby. Yes, that was it, I thought. It rang true. He cradled the ruby-red blooms like a child. He took his place in line, behind me. His cheeks were flushed and his hair stuck up a bit at the crown.

The person in line ahead of me was an elderly man in a flannel shirt and zip-up vest. He seemed annoyed as he checked his watch. The cashier announced his total and he responded by handing her a clutch of dollar bills before digging in the lining of his vest for coins. Quickly, Giles Owita supplied some change from a pocket of his apron. He said something to the elderly man that I couldn't hear, but whatever it was it seemed to loosen some knot of tension in the older man's shoulders.

A teenage girl with smoke-colored eye shadow and a butterfly tattoo on her wrist had taken her place behind the man with the roses. She was quick to offer a coin to the cause herself. "Here," she said to the guy with the roses. He put the quarters in my hand and I played my role in the chain by passing them along. The elderly man's narrow face took on a smoother and more pleasant look. After that, it seemed to me that we were all connected—me and Giles Owita; a seemingly gruff old man; a young girl with purple hair and a silver nose ring; a man rushing off to some important event in his life; and even my typically cranky neighbor, who was now extending a hand into the air as if to say she needed assistance.

Oh, goodness. I hoped she wasn't barking some sort of order at Giles Owita. She could be quite ill-tempered.

A moment passed before I realized—she was simply greeting someone.

Me.

Her neighbor. Remember, Carol?

I waved back.

"How are you?" I said, trying to hide my surprise that she was being so friendly. She closed the space between us with a few eager steps and I noticed the lovely auburn highlights in her hair. It tumbled freely, brushing her cheekbones.

"It's hard to shop with a baby on your hip," she said.

"Oh, honey. I know. I've been there. Three times over. But you look great, because all mothers of beautiful babies look great."

I tickled her baby on his foot and he giggled. The neighbor mom seemed happy as she left. I placed my items on the counter, one by one. Giles Owita didn't seem aware that I was studying him as the cashier, Marie, made stabs at chitchat. I answered her remarks about the weather and a flavor of coffee creamer I'd picked out. This close to him, I noticed once again the aura of calm that seemed to surround Giles Owita. It was something I felt, but couldn't explain. Finally, I spoke my first words to him. "Don't I recognize you?"

I swiped my debit card, and Giles Owita looked quizzically toward me, but not directly at me. He lowered his eyebrows, concentrating.

"You're Giles Owita," I said, as if he didn't know.

"Yes. I'm Giles," he said. "Have we met?"

Time seemed to slow as I extended my hand. I took note

of every detail in the way he shook it, managing a mix of gentleness and firmness in his grip. Again, he didn't look me in the eye.

Marie folded a stick of Juicy Fruit into her mouth and studied us both intently. I watched as Giles Owita stacked my six-packs of cola and ginger ale in a paper bag. Another customer added herself to the line behind the girl with the purple hair.

"I'm Sarah Driscoll's neighbor. Carol Wall," I said. "You left me a note today. We missed each other, though. I'm sorry, and I . . ."

His face lit up with a smile. "How are you, Mrs. Wall?"

And that was when my good intentions fell by the wayside. Suddenly I'd forgotten about my pledge to just introduce myself like a normal person. While Giles Owita had managed to put everyone else on our grocery line at ease, his remarkable calm had the effect on me—in this moment at least—of rendering me awkward and unsure of myself, graceless in the face of such grace. "I'll make this really quick," I said. "The next time you come to my yard, I'd like to be there and give you a tour. There's a list I'm working on, and I want to go over it with you. Maybe if you call me, we could set a time at your convenience."

"All right." He nodded. "We live out near the airport, but my travels often take me past your house. You have a lovely compound, Mrs. Wall."

I searched the depths of my purse and with a quick, apologetic glance at those in line, I hastily retrieved Giles Owita's letter, unfolded the page, and showed him the sentence that gave me pause the first time I'd read it.

"I have only this one concern," I said, tapping the page with an index finger as he began to lift my bags of groceries into the waiting cart.

He leaned closer to look. Seeing his own note, inscribed with the distinctive, right-leaning script that flowed from his pen, he flashed his million-dollar smile. Instantly charmed, I began to feel a melting of resolve.

"Those azaleas at your compound will be beautiful," Giles Owita said. "Soon, we are going to see their deep pink blooms."

Oh, Good Lord.

"They only lack some helpful chemicals," Giles Owita cheerfully informed me. "Which I can easily supply from my garden shed, as noted here."

Far back in the line, someone said, "Let's get a move on."

I was embarrassed by this, and yet undeterred. "I have this quirk," I said, my nerves on edge. "I've never liked azaleas. I hope you aren't too disappointed."

Giles Owita looked regretful, but accepting. "What time would be best for me to visit you, Mrs. Wall?"

Thank God. He was going to cooperate with no more arguing, however polite. And I would no longer have to live with azaleas.

Before I could set the time for our meeting, the new store manager stepped in. I recognized him from the oversized poster in the entrance, one that rather unattractively showed every line and pore on his ruddy face. He was in his early forties, and his broad shoulders stretched his fitted button-down shirt.

"Why don't you help this nice young lady out to her car?" he said to Giles Owita, all the while looking at anyone and everyone *but* Giles. "I'll take your place here, buddy-boy."

"Buddy-boy?" I found myself repeating with a frown. "You're kidding—right?"

"It's what I call my son, and he's an honor student!" the manager proclaimed.

I looked around me, as if to say, *Can you believe this?* The others waiting in line seemed to disapprove as well, but they didn't speak up. Our moment of togetherness and connection had evaporated. They fidgeted and frowned as if they agreed with me but didn't want to make a scene.

If Giles Owita shared my anger, he didn't show it. I was amazed to see the way he pulled his shoulders back to stand more proudly.

"Look, if you want to blame someone for the delay . . ." I said to the manager.

But he pointedly directed his attention toward the next customer in the line. Giles Owita stepped away from the station. He retied his Foodland apron for a neater fit. His movements were measured and unhurried. Meanwhile, I fumbled and stewed. I grasped my receipt and turned away from Marie without offering the customary pleasantries. I felt my cheeks grow red. I slapped the folded letter back into my purse, along with my receipt. Being called "buddy-boy" was probably the least of the insults that a person of color had to endure in a place like Roanoke, and yet Giles Owita seemed at peace. His hands gripped my grocery cart. "Are you ready to go, Mrs. Wall?"

Outside, the rain had stopped. We stepped off the sidewalk.

"I'm sorry," I said. "I should have spoken with you at a later time."

"It is okay. You shouldn't worry."

I stole a glance at him. To my ears, his pronunciation of "okay" sounded more like "okee," which lent a hopeful, lilting tone each time he spoke the word. His steps were quick. It was a challenge for me to keep up. I hoped he didn't notice how I struggled, taking double steps to help match his pace.

"It's just that I wanted to schedule a time for the yard," I said. "So I could be there to show you around."

If I'd been truly honest, I might have added: *And so I could be there to make sure you ripped out those azaleas.*

"For the record," I continued, "what happened back there with your boss wasn't right. We're not all rednecks here in Roanoke. I promise. I hope you'll give us another chance to be more welcoming."

He nodded, unperturbed, and said nothing. I shuddered to imagine what he thought of us. "How long have you lived here?"

"In Roanoke? About two years. My wife is a nurse at Valley Hospital. We moved here for the job, which also led to a job for me, in the hospital kitchen. When I was laid off several weeks ago, imagine my good fortune in finding two excellent part-time positions. This one opened up at Foodland, and then, as you know, I have been able to assist at the Garden Shoppe. From there, I've begun to pick up landscaping jobs, like yours. Many, many people have been welcoming to us, these past two years. We like it very much in Roanoke."

"Well, I'm glad to hear that," I said. It seemed that Giles Owita was trying to console me, as if it were me who had been insulted, and not him.

"There are many interruptions at the checkout counter," he continued. "This man they have put in charge of the store lacks patience. Something like this happens almost every day. Yesterday, he chased a very small boy—I believe he was Pakistani—who had opened a box of Pop-Tarts. The mother was screaming in protest. She had a cart spilling over with groceries, and had been too busy spending money in this man's store to notice her child's very minor misbehavior. I'm afraid that she tossed a few items at the manager. First, there was a bottle of ketchup. Next, some rolls of paper towels. Yet not one of us stepped in to help that man. Not even when the lady pushed her cart at him several times, like a bull charging. The manager was unhurt, but she succeeded in making a very big point. In the end, he retreated to his office, where he was instantly busy with some papers on his desk. We were amused to see him through the glass. He did not once look up at us. We took much joy in this, and felt it justified."

I laughed out loud, which clearly pleased Giles Owita.

"Would next Saturday afternoon be okay?" he said.

"Next Saturday?"

"For the tour of your compound."

"Oh. Right. Yes." I thought out loud for a moment. "That's the day after my parents are moving to a new assisted living facility. They have lived in the same house for more than fifty years. This is a difficult move for them, and I want to help them get adjusted. How about three o'clock?"

"Three o'clock will be fine," he said.

So, this much was settled. We had a time, a place, and some notion of the tasks at hand. Above us, clouds shifted and mingled as they made their way toward the perimeter of a brisk Southern night. The silver moon, three-quarters full, floated above us. Lights from passing cars shone on the rain-slick surface of the parking lot. The reflections made me think of comets stretching their elongated tails.

"When you stop by," I said, "do you think you could help me select something else to put in place of the azaleas?"

His eyes lit up.

"All right. I'll think on this."

I suddenly remembered something. "Oh, wait. Your fee? You didn't say."

"Ten dollars per hour."

We reached my van, and I turned to him. "So little? Are you sure? It really does not seem enough."

"It's my standard rate."

So many odd jobs, worked for minimum wage. It occurred to me that Giles Owita must not have any credentials beyond a green card, and I found myself wondering how he managed to obtain one of those. Yet Sarah said he was the hardest worker they'd ever had at the Garden Shoppe. Dick would be so pleased I'd hired him, I told myself. I opened the hatch and then stood aside to watch Giles Owita tuck the bags inside, one by one.

"You say you live near the airport?" I asked, hoping to somehow find out more about him.

"Yes. My wife and I, and our two sons. We're on Overland Street, on the north part of town."

"Overland. Right. I know that area. It's close to the expressway and not far from where I teach." What neither of us said was that Overland was across town from where I lived. Roanoke is a historically segregated community, like much of the South, and had been recently listed as among the nation's most segregated areas. Overland was somewhat of an anomaly. It was a neighborhood filled with modest homes and was an integrated community. I think the expressway and construction of another major road was responsible for this progress. I never was sure who had managed that feat of civil (and social) engineering, or if that was even one of the goals of the construction.

He nodded.

"Sarah may have told you I'm a high school English teacher," I said, still trying to make conversation.

"No. We do not talk much at work."

"Dick and I also have two sons. With a daughter in between. We used to call her our rose between two thorns. I know it's silly, but . . ."

"Silly? I don't think so."

The end of his sentence dovetailed with the increasingly loud roar of a jet passing overhead. We paused to watch it as it crossed, left to right, through the sky above us. It seemed almost to float as it approached Wildwood Mountain. Giles Owita was especially intent in tracking its progress, craning his neck at an awkward angle. Yet there was something cautionary in the way he soberly searched the sky, and I refrained from saying anything more. The set of his jaw was firm, as if holding back deep emotion. Questions flooded my mind. How old were his sons? Had they been born in Kenya? What brought the family to the States? But most of all, I wanted to ask him why he seemed so sad right now, as he watched the jet that streaked the sky.

As if he read my thoughts, he said, "We, too, have a daughter. She is in Kenya, and waits to be brought over. There are complications with her visa. She is our firstborn child. You see, my wife and I . . ."

I waited for more detail. He hesitated. This time, I pressed ahead. "What is your daughter's name?"

"Her name is Lok. Her favorite flower is the rose. You have given me a thought, Mrs. Wall. She, too, must be our rose among the many thorns of life. Yes. That's it. My wife will like it." Giles Owita looked wistful.

"I'm glad you like my metaphor," I said. "And I just have this feeling Lok will be here soon."

At that moment it seemed to me that he slammed the hatch a bit too hard, like a period to mark the end of our conversation. I circled the van and climbed into the driver's seat. Behind me, other people's cars slashed by and Giles Owita stood ready to advise me on backing out.

I rolled down the window.

"Wabironenore," he said as I passed by.

"Wabir-o-ne-nore," I carefully repeated. "It means goodbye?"

"It does," Giles Owita said. "But also, we will see each other later."

4.

A Promising Blade of Grass

It hadn't been easy to convince my parents to move out of our family home and into an assisted living facility nearby. Mama had finally given in, though. She was having some sort of problem that increasingly affected her gait, and she also realized that she could no longer safely handle my father's worsening Alzheimer's on her own.

I knew what my parents' move would mean for me. As the daughter who was geographically the closest, I'd be the one to shoulder most of the burden of overseeing their move and settling them in. I'd be the one shopping for them and making sure they were well taken care of. In truth, though, taking care of my parents wasn't new to me. I'd always felt my parents needed me. Even as a little girl, I'd felt responsible for their happiness.

I had a sister—an older sister—named Barbara. She was born "mongoloid," as they called Down syndrome babies in those days, and today doctors might have been able to fix the defective valve in her heart. Back then, it wasn't possible, and when she was just two years old she died. I was only seven months old at the time, so I had no memories of her. All I had were the pictures of her that I'd seen around the house.

The cause of Barbara's death was always kept vague (at least to me and my younger sister, Judy). We were only told that she had a heart problem. I think most children know when something is being hidden from them—something so big—and I was perhaps even more sensitive than most. There seemed to be a shadow of mystery around my sister and her death, especially where my mother was concerned. Daddy didn't mind talking about Barbara, and often when we were alone he'd bring her up. Daddy always called her "our little angel." But Mama was a different story, and the unspoken rule around our house was that Barbara could never be brought up in front of Mama, nor could Mama know that Daddy talked about her to us when she wasn't around.

Maybe that was why I was always described as such a grown-up child. I had sharply attuned antennae for sadness of any kind, especially anything that touched Mama. She was a wonderful mother in so many ways, but I learned early on that once riled, her anger could be a powerful thing. As an adult, I realized that this was a side effect of her enormous sadness and guilt over Barbara, and her disappointment at not having been able to have a house full of children. After my younger sister was born, she was told she could have no more, and I think that loss, combined with her grief over Barbara, limited her happiness forever after. But of course I knew none of this as a child. Back then, I just knew that it was my job to help Daddy keep Mama calm and reasonably content.

My radar for anything involving Barbara, and Barbara's effect on Mama, was bizarrely acute. I remember once when I was five or six years old, I overheard a phone conversation Mama was having with one of her distant relatives. Mama and she must not have spoken in a while because they were swapping vital statistics. I remember Mama saying, "Yes, Carol is six and Judy is four. And our Barbara died in 1952." I knew all of this, but then came the part I did not understand at all. Mama said, "Well, you know she was a mongoloid." I had no idea what that word meant, but something told me that it had to be something really bad. And from then on it became my project to find out more. This wasn't just nosiness, it felt to me like a vital responsibility. Because how could I protect my mother if I didn't know what I was protecting her from?

Not long after that, I started to put all the pieces together. I figured out that when Daddy asked me if I wanted to ride along with him while he ran an errand, this meant that he wanted to talk about Barbara. Daddy was just bursting with grief, and sometimes it overflowed. He told me how he used to take drives with Barbara, and he'd sing to her and she'd cock her head and look at him, almost as if she understood. I remember he said once, "You know that Barbara was the kind of child who never grows up."

Perhaps this was where I first got the idea that there were two kinds of people in this world—those who take care of others, and those who needed taking care of themselves. I always figured I was the first kind. Then, after my cancer diagnosis, I had spent too long feeling like the second kind. It was only recently that I'd learned we are all the same. But I'm getting ahead of myself.

I've never been sure, but I think that after Barbara died Mama and Daddy moved me into her room. It would have made sense, since it was the nicest room and now I was the oldest. As a child, I lay in that room thinking about Barbara and wondered if she was looking for me, the same way I was looking for her. One of the photos of Barbara that I often studied also included me—I am maybe four months old, lying on my back on the sofa. In the foreground is Barbara in a little walker. She paused and is looking at me as if to say, "Well, let's see, who is that?" Or at least that's what I imagined she was thinking. I did a lot of filling in of the blanks as a child. I think that's how I got to be such a storyteller. No one was telling me anything, so I had to come up with a narrative of my own.

I was a child who often grew lost and frightened by my own thoughts. When I was getting to an age when I was starting to think about boys, I became very troubled by some of the images that were coming into my mind. I was raised to be a good girl, and these thoughts and feelings I was having seemed wrong. So I went to Mama, and I told her with great earnestness that I was having some bad thoughts about men and women. Mama looked at me and said, "You know what, Carol? What you're thinking and feeling is normal. My minister told me that you can't keep the birds from flying over your head, but you can keep them from building a nest there." I found that advice so reassuring, and I tried to apply it so many times over the years—not always successfully. Mama wasn't able to take her own advice either. Sometimes it seemed that all of Mama's guilt and sadness had built a permanent structure in her head.

Mama had a strange way of coping with Barbara's death, and it often came out in a weird sort of gallows humor. There was a story she loved to tell, as if it were the funniest thing in the world. Although she usually completely avoided the subject of Barbara and her death, this was the one weird exception. She told the story over and over, and I learned to know when it was coming. Apparently, at Barbara's funeral, after my sister's little white casket had been lowered into the ground, my grandfather held me in his arms nearby and he tripped, nearly sending us both tumbling into the grave. This recollection always made Mama laugh. It just tickled her to death. Of course, the effect it had on me was altogether different. I found myself obsessing over what might have happened if we had really fallen in. How would I have gotten out?

That wasn't the only thing that troubled me about Barbara's grave. There was a photograph that deeply affected me. I found it one day when I was digging around in a drawer, no doubt searching for answers. It wasn't long after that overheard phone call. In the photo, Barbara's tiny coffin is resting just above the grave, waiting to be lowered. Around it are heaps and heaps of flowers. The image was black and white, but in my mind I imagined that the colorful petals were already wilting. At night, I tried to visualize the reds and purples, pinks and yellows pictured there, and even to count their blooms. Suddenly, I understood in a way that I never had before that they'd buried my sister, there in the ground, beneath the soil.

Daddy took Judy and me to Barbara's grave, often in May, the month that Barbara was born. Mama never came, and it was understood that she'd be too sad to join us. Each time we visited, I placed some fresh-picked flowers on her grave. I knew even then that just like those flowers in the picture, the flowers that I left on Barbara's grave would wilt and die. Was it any wonder that I never liked flowers? I preferred green things that grew in the ground, things that never bloomed only to fade.

We lived in a house of secret sadness. By the time I was a teenager I knew this as well as I knew my own name. But I wouldn't find out until I was already married that there was one massive, as yet untold, secret that directly involved me in a terrifying way.

It went back to when I was just a baby, in the months before Barbara died. I was five months old, and apparently I had an awful case of colic. I screamed and cried all the time. My parents, no doubt already exhausted from coping with Barbara's profound needs, now had two babies who cried for them all the time. Our regular pediatrician was serving in Korea, so they sought the advice of a doctor who was known for some innovative new therapies. It was his theory that I had an enlarged thymus, and that was causing swelling, which resulted in discomfort and crying. So he recommended three full treatments of radiation to my thymus gland.

To make matters worse, the radiation treatments given at the time weren't targeted, and the entire upper part of my body was exposed to the radiation. Mama later told me that when our regular doctor returned from Korea, he shouted, "These treatments will kill her one day!" I can only imagine how she must have wept, her universe collapsing again.

When I was eleven, I had my first non-cancerous lump removed. I had no fear, and my parents certainly didn't tell me the cause. I was just told that I had a little something in my neck and the doctor would remove it. By the time I was seventeen, the lump had grown back and I was sent to a different surgeon. Again, I don't recall being scared and I think that's because I wasn't allowed to be. There wasn't enough room in our lives for all of Mama's anxiety, let alone adding any of my own. I was terribly sick in the hospital, but because Mama was so upset about the situation, Daddy would leave me alone there and take Mama home.

I don't know if Mama and Daddy would ever have told me about the radiation if it hadn't been for an article they read about increased cancer risks in adults who'd been subjected to radiation treatments as babies. I vividly remember their call. I was twenty-one, already married to Dick, and when the telephone rang I was ironing one of his shirts (probably the one and only time in our entire marriage that I did such a thing). Mama and Daddy were on separate extensions, and they were obviously upset. Picking up on their emotions as I always did, I became shaken myself and by the time I hung up the phone I was crying. I told Dick what they'd said—that there seemed to be an incubation period of about twenty-five years, and if you passed that without a cancer diagnosis, then it probably wasn't going to cause any more trouble. Dick said, "So we can keep a check on that. It doesn't sound so horrible."

When Dick said that, I thought, *Do people actually grow up in homes where they approach life with such optimism?* I had always pretended to be optimistic for my mother's sake, but I wasn't actually an optimistic person. In truth, I pretty much always expected disaster. But I knew better than to show that fear to the world. I knew that when I wasn't light and happy, bad things happened.

Not long after the first lump was removed from my neck, I started developing terrible headaches that I eventually learned were migraines. I was twelve years old, and one morning before school I was sitting at the breakfast table and Daddy said, "Carol, on the way to school we're going to run by the emergency room."

I had my homemade banners for the football game all around me, and I looked up at Daddy, wondering why on earth I needed to go to the hospital.

Clearly uncomfortable, his eyes darting around the room, he

said, "Your mother wants you to have a head X-ray because you've been having so many headaches."

I could have put up a fight and insisted I was okay and that I wanted to go straight to school. But I went along without complaint because I knew it was easier to mollify Mama's fears than to contradict them. And of course it turned out that nothing was wrong.

The result of all of this quiet sadness and outsized anxiety was that I was truly at a loss for how to respond appropriately to anything emotional. On the one hand, I was relieved that Dick didn't run around in a panic after my parents' phone call and shove me into a waiting ambulance. But on the other hand, I never felt entitled to feel scared on my own behalf.

Each time I received a new diagnosis or potentially frightening news, I wasn't allowed to run to my mother for comfort the way other women might have. Instead, my first thought had to be how I could minimize the bad news so as to spare my parents further pain. A therapist once told me that I was like a person who got shot and tried to wipe up my own blood before the photographers arrived.

When I was little, I used to fantasize about the day I was born and how happy my parents must have been. So much of my self-worth came from my ability to mitigate their grief—and the only way I could do that was by being perfect and never causing them worry. But cancer proved once and for all that I was not the perfect baby my parents had hoped for. I was damaged goods.

· · ·

It was Saturday, the day after my parents' move to an assisted living home, Heathwood Hearth. I sat on my kitchen floor, surrounded by boxes of their things that wouldn't fit in their new apartment. There was so much of it—decades' worth of memories mixed in with stuff that either had to be thrown away or donated. As much as I wanted to help them with this truly depressing task, the whole thing made me sad and angry.

The move had gone smoothly enough. The admissions director welcomed my parents personally and gave them a tour that began in the two-story grand foyer and ended in the dining room, where lemonade and oatmeal cookies still warm from the oven were served. My mother was pleased to see the nurses' station and the bank of elevators quite near their apartment.

Early in the day, a pleasant, gray-haired nurse presented Daddy with his special bracelet, designed to set off an alarm if Daddy tried to exit the building. The nurse cleverly explained it was "something like what you wore overseas, in service, to get in the chow line," upon which Daddy squared his shoulders and offered his wrist without hesitation. I thought for a moment that he was going to give a soldier's proud salute. After this he wandered up and down the corridors, as if on patrol.

Daddy was much safer here, and Mama was, too, but there was no getting around how sad this day was for Mama. She probably could have held on to the house if it weren't for Daddy's illness. But he'd taken to wandering any time of the day or night, not to mention remarking on the size of women's breasts. It was a startling development in a man who'd always been so gentlemanly.

My mother, even at eighty, was a smart, determined woman who could still put on airs of Scarlett at the barbecue if the situation called for it. It never failed to amuse me how, right in the middle of a conversation with someone, she'd excuse herself and leave the room. Then, after a minute or two, she'd return with freshened lipstick and hair. Mama could be fragile, as well I knew, but she was strong-willed, too, and it was obvious as the day wore on that this move had knocked the wind out of her. Mama and I spent the afternoon hanging some family photos on the walls of their apartment—or rather I hung while she directed me where to put things. Gradually, her enthusiasm fully drained away, and by early afternoon, she surrendered to a nap. I tiptoed out to go home and then collapsed on my own bed.

Today, I had returned to have lunch with them. My mother's angry words an hour earlier were still ringing in my ears.

"Just wait till you get old," she whispered fiercely as she stabbed a bite of chicken with her fork. "You'll see. A person's home is everything."

"I hope I get to *be* old, Mama," I snapped back. Then I felt guilty for reminding her of their innocent mistake that couldn't be changed. I had so aspired to being the perfect daughter in this situation, but apparently it didn't take much for me to lose my poise. I wished that I'd been able to bite my tongue and remind myself that Mama was only angry at me because there wasn't anyone else to be angry at. She couldn't blame Daddy for being sick. And even if she could, he was way past absorbing blame.

While Mama and I seethed over our meals, my father chewed his smothered chicken with mechanical precision. Swallowing mouthfuls of food and taking big, sloppy slurps of his coffee were all he seemed to care about. In the life before Alzheimer's struck, he had always played the role of mediator and protector for my mother. Now he looked at both of us as if we were strangers he had encountered at a bus stop.

I reached into another of the boxes on my kitchen floor, flinging the top carelessly in the direction of the trash can. I was surprised to find a large black-and-white photo from my parents' square dance days. I used to watch Mama and Daddy dancing with their wholesome group of friends on a summer night on the flagstone patio outside my bedroom window. I was sometimes allowed to join the grown-ups for bowls of homemade vanilla ice cream studded with nuggets of strawberries or fresh peaches, and they would pretend not to know I was up past my bedtime. I felt the joy of this as if it had happened last night.

During this walk down memory lane, I suddenly heard the ring of the doorbell. I jumped, as if I were just waiting for bad news. I pictured Daddy on the lam, having found my house with the help of a series of strangers. I imagined him striding into my foyer to announce that he was going back to Radford *right this very instant*, and he wanted his car keys given back to him at once.

My rational mind took over and I checked the clock on

the microwave: 2:56. It was time for my meeting with Giles Owita.

I thought I had left a larger window of time for feeling sorry for myself. Instead, I splashed water on my face and pulled a comb through my hair as Rhudy trotted toward the foyer, issuing more of his "happy barks of warning." I snatched an unused marble notebook I had found at the bottom of a box that morning. I also grabbed the list I'd made.

I opened the front door and rearranged my face into a pleasant look, but was surprised to find no one standing on our porch. I put Rhudy on the leash and stepped outside. On either side of me were sadly sagging boxwoods and no Giles Owita. A bright blue Neon was parked at Sarah's house. Its driver was AWOL. Maybe I had imagined the doorbell ringing.

"Hello?" I called out.

Silence.

I closed my eyes. A gentle breeze lifted my hair. Soon a reedy, snapping sound floated toward me from the left side of the house where the azaleas were. Could Giles Owita have rung the doorbell simply to announce his arrival? Had he already plunged his shovel into the moistened earth to leverage an azalea from its hold in the ground, even as I looked for him?

As I walked along, I pictured the stubborn roots giving way, but not without a fight. I was happy to think of Giles Owita applying all his strength, acting on my request and then waiting for me to join him to discuss different options. Or maybe he was planning a surprise. I didn't want to spoil the moment, but perhaps he didn't realize how long it would surely take him to dig up just one of those azaleas with their deep-reaching, fibrous roots.

When Rhudy rounded the corner of the house, the mystery was solved. He gave a single, urgent bark and entered his version of a pointer's stance. Soon I caught up with him, and oh, dear. It was Giles Owita, all right, wearing his navy work suit and occupied with the azaleas, as I'd hoped. But the shrubs were hardly under full assault. In fact, Giles Owita lovingly tended to the first azalea with fingers that carefully plucked away the crisp, dead leaves and dried debris that had fallen from the overhanging trees. His feet were planted firmly on the sloping, moss-covered ground, and his eyes were warm with concern as he inspected the healthy green parts now becoming visible on the azalea. On some level, I realized I should have been grateful for these efforts. Secretly, though, I felt like the birthday girl whose candles had been blown out by a darting guest whose mother hadn't taught him proper party etiquette. Any gratitude I might have felt for Giles Owita's hard work dissolved into frustration and bubbling anger. I hated azaleas, and I was entitled to hate them. I wanted them out of my yard, and I was paying this man to remove them. What could he be thinking right now? Did he actually believe he was there to follow some internal drive to minister to each and every plant on earth and make it healthier?

Absurd.

I saw two plastic containers sitting on the ground beside the shrubbery. It was even worse than I'd thought, because a nozzle was attached to each, for spraying. These must have been the chemicals that he had referred to in his letter.

Was he being defiant? Or had he been merely pretending to understand when I told him what I wanted?

I pointed at the buckets and tried to keep my voice steady. "Fertilizer?"

"Yes, and an anti-fungal," Giles Owita informed me in his earnest way. "Your plants are in need of both. But soon they will be blossoming!" Then he offered me a smile that was like a sunrise—and all of my anger and petty annoyance melted away.

This wasn't anything to get angry about, I told myself. I just needed to be clear, to assert myself. This man was my employee, after all, and I shouldn't have to be shy about having things done my way.

"I thought we agreed those shrubs are coming out," I said in the firmest, clearest voice I could muster. "All three of them. Remember? I've never liked azaleas, as I think you know by now. They're pretty on a golf course, maybe, but at home, the blossoms don't last long and when you try to cut them back . . ." My speech trailed off and I found I had nothing left to say. Giles Owita looked blankly in my general direction.

I was sure we'd moved beyond the tipping point about the azaleas. I bit my lip, trying to call back the anger I'd felt a moment before. I should have been able to conjure it again, after all I was completely justified. But when I tried, the feeling didn't even start to happen. There was something so innocent and endearing about this man who worked so eagerly. Or was he simply clever? Charming? Stubborn?

Endless seconds passed. Giles Owita maintained his stance, with one foot planted in a spot between the brittle branches of that first azalea, and the other settled firmly on a patch of the soggy moss that always seemed to flourish on this side of our house. A Leyland cypress separated us from the smaller house next door. As I looked up into the feathery limbs, I thought of Sarah Driscoll's perfectly landscaped yard and of all the other yards on our street. Dick and I had a mess here. Maybe I had to relinquish control and let Giles Owita prescribe the solutions. I had the sudden fleeting, illogical thought that this moment with Giles Owita in my yard was something that I had been waiting for all of my life.

Still, I wavered. Stay firm, or give in?

Giles Owita glanced up at me. Concern was etched across his brow. He was going to plead his case, I feared. ("They will be beautiful!" I could almost hear him say.) *Don't let him win,* I told myself. *Stick to your guns.*

"How are your parents doing in their new apartment, Mrs. Wall? My wife and I have prayed they would weather their move with a minimum of stress."

I took in a sharp breath.

My parents? Giles Owita had time to pray for someone else's parents?

I searched his face. He was either utterly sincere, or a very good actor. I took a small step back, but my foot began to slide as Rhudy's leash zipped through my fingers. I started to fall. The azalea trembled as Giles Owita leaped to grab me by the elbow. My right hand grasped the sleeve of his navy work suit and my other hand found the roughness of brick on the side of my house. It was one of the few times I would ever touch Giles Owita.

"Oh. Thank you. I almost fell." I let go of his sleeve. My balance had been restored, but my pulse was still racing. Rhudy was pacing nervously nearby, the purple leash trailing behind him. "You and your wife have prayed for my parents? That's so kind. I'm humbled." My voice broke as I said the word *parents*, and I thought of them grieving yet another loss in their long life together.

"It is our joy to pray for them," Giles Owita said.

He seemed so sincere. I searched his earnest expression for signs of cynicism or duplicity. He continued staring off into the distance.

"I appreciate those prayers," I said, "and I've been praying for Lok." I added the last part with a liar's special emphasis on every word. But even as I said it, I suddenly knew that I needed it to be true, and I resolved to get down on my knees on the subject, starting tomorrow, at Mass. "Was there any news of her this week?"

He shook his head. I gazed up again at the Leyland cypress and tried to conjure the delicate shape of the face of a faraway daughter who loved roses.

"Do you have a picture I could see?" I asked.

"At our house, there are many pictures. I will try to remember to bring one with me, next time. Our Lok is a beautiful girl. We have treasured her, from the day she arrived."

"Of course," I said. "I'm sure you have. Is there anything Dick and I can do to help? He's a lawyer, you know. So, if you decide . . ."

"We will continue to wait and hope," he said.

As I stood there watching him, Giles Owita continued his work on the azaleas, and I decided to let him do as he wished with them without further fight. His work on the second bush went quickly. He didn't seem to mind that I hovered close by while he pinched off debris to find the healthy parts. I took advantage of the chance to ask him further questions about his family. He told me that his wife's name was Bienta. His expression brightened as he spoke of her. They were of the Luo tribe, second largest of more than forty tribes in Kenya. Bienta's name was "a Luo-cized version," as he put it, of the French name Bernadette.

"She was born on the mainland, near Kisumu," he explained. "While I was brought into the world in more rural circumstances on the tiny island of Rusinga, in Lake Victoria."

"Well, I hope to meet Bienta soon," I said.

"You will," he quickly agreed. "Sometime, I will bring her by your compound. She is reserved and proper, but not shy."

My envious nature bubbled up to the surface. I wondered if Dick ever wore such an adoring look when he spoke about me. I felt deflated to recall a petty argument we had had not long ago. We'd screamed at each other until our faces were red. Dick had made another of his misty-eyed comments to me about how many life lessons we had learned from my cancer treatment. Instantly, I'd wanted to slap him silly. We made up in the end— we always did—but no one won, and nothing, really, was resolved. In counterpoint, and as a form of self-torture, I imagined Giles Owita and Bienta holding hands before a meal. Their boys (as I pictured them) sat opposite. They all bowed their heads in prayer. Their house was small, but well kept. Roses magically bloomed at the door in all seasons. As they repeated their so-far-unanswered prayers for Lok, they remained generous of spirit, concerned for other people. I thought of Paul's letter to the Galatians, where he instructed that we should "not grow weary in doing good." The Owitas clearly did not tire of doing good. In fact, they took the time to lift two strangers, my struggling parents, to the tender mercy of God above.

Then I found myself wondering something. "Your Luo tribe has its own religion, true?"

Giles Owita seemed unhurried and relaxed, as if completely open to a teaching moment, even as our other projects waited. In fact, he looked pleased at this invitation to revisit the way of life he learned as a child. I brought him a bottle of water from the house and he paused in his work for a moment.

"Tribal beliefs are based on a reverence for ancestors," Giles Owita began. "In our culture, the elderly, whether living or deceased, are revered. We're taught that our ancestors live below"—he pointed to the ground—"and are our foundation. From this place, they offer special wisdom. If I were to dream about my father, I would not say I dreamed *about* him, but rather, that my father *has brought a dream.* Our ancestors are still actors in our lives, a source of wisdom and protection. Such dreams are shared with others in the village, with everyone giving an interpretation. In my father's time, some food and drink would even be sprinkled on the ground before a meal. Given the state of medical care and the fact that disease and death are commonplace in our part of the world, it is considered an achievement to have reached the stage of life your parents have attained, Mrs. Wall."

Like a concert pianist concluding the second movement of a flawless performance, Giles Owita lifted his hands from the leafy depths of the second azalea. As if on cue, a dull gray station wagon poked its dusty nose over the crest of Mount Vernon Road. It proceeded down the gentle grade in its usual painstaking way and the brake lights flashed repeatedly as if the vehicle's shock absorbers were being tested.

Oh, my God. Not him, I thought.

"Don't forget about that third azalea," I prompted desperately, hoping to keep Giles Owita from noticing the dusty car and its irascible driver.

It was someone we all knew well and watched out for, the Reverend Gerald Jacks, a longtime widower. He was a Lutheran minister, retired, a neighbor from two streets over. His children, who lived away, had crept cautiously into town to give him a lavish eightieth birthday party several years ago, and then headed back to the West Coast, where they seemed to be hiding out. Their reticence was understandable, their father being one of those intimidating people who seemed destined to hold his power to the grave. His thatch of white hair took the shape of flames licking up from the pit of hell, and no one in the neighborhood had ever seen him without his thick black glasses. They magnified his unruly salt-and-pepper eyebrows and emphasized the harshness of his pale blue, peering eyes.

As the dusty station wagon crept along, the Reverend Jacks made a point to leer at Giles Owita. This rudeness happened just as I knew it would, and I felt responsible and helpless, all at once. Yet given how he'd responded to a similar insult from his manager at the grocery store, I wasn't surprised when Giles Owita turned the other cheek with a respectful nod.

"He must be a relative of your boss at the supermarket," I quipped halfheartedly. I noticed that Giles Owita's eyes held a twinkle in response.

Reverend Jacks had truly tested my patience over the years. When our older son, Chad, was learning to drive, he was merciless in riding Chad's bumper or tooting the horn to point out any small mistake. Far more unforgivable, he became the only person in the neighborhood who cast a menacing eye toward Phil's young basketball teammates, especially those of color.

"Could you believe that when a pair of hedge clippers went missing from that man's garage, the reverend called our house and asked me if any of Phil's 'colored' friends had been around that afternoon?"

"Yes. I could believe," Giles Owita answered calmly.

"I gave Reverend Jacks a piece of my mind, with no holding back," I continued. "I called him a racist and a sinner, and asked him what on earth anyone would want with his rusty clippers. Later on, he found the clippers in the shrubbery, where he himself had left them when the sun became too much for him."

Giles Owita clucked his tongue.

"At least he called to let us know," I said as Giles Owita turned back to his work. "Perhaps I should give him credit for that. Growing old is an accomplishment, as you have said."

"It is more difficult to contain our hurts when others are affected," Giles Owita observed. "We are prone to speak out on their behalf, as you did for me, that evening at the store. That is a good thing, I believe. I certainly appreciated it, and told my wife about it. Such times can be lonely. There are times when no one is assumed to be a friend."

"You must have had to confront that kind of bigoted, disrespectful treatment more than I can possibly imagine," I said.

He gave a gentle shrug. "Most people are very nice, and the ones who aren't, you can tell from the first time you meet them."

At last he put the finishing touches on the third azalea. Then he pulled a white protective mask from the pocket of his work suit and slipped it on. His eyes shone brightly as he motioned that, for safety's sake, I should step away. With Rhudy, I retreated to the top of the slight incline where I was content to sit on the grass, a safe distance away from where Giles Owita sprayed his chemicals. It amazed me the way he'd managed to find fulfillment in a world far removed from everything he most likely knew and loved as a boy. It was odd, but sitting in the grass in my own front yard, I felt a bit transported, too. My various lists seemed less important. What I needed was patience.

I tipped my face to the sky and breathed in deeply. Maybe it wasn't just an excuse that Dick and I had been too busy with other things—such as raising our children and helping our parents—to care for our yard. Maybe we weren't so awfully lazy as I not-so-secretly feared. Perhaps we were worthy people who were just a little scatterbrained. Perfect or not, in its present state, this tiny green slice of longitude and latitude was meant to be ours and had potential for beauty.

Perhaps it wasn't too late.

I hadn't thought so optimistically in a while.

My gaze fell on a single, promising blade of grass. Giles Owita was only slightly out of focus in the background. Maybe it truly was part of his mission in life, to work on each and every plant he encountered and make it healthier. And maybe that wasn't so absurd.

What if this elegant Kenyan man with his knack for flowers was part of a larger plan for God's work in the world? Would I dare to thwart that effort?

It was a stunning and sweepingly illogical line of thought. As I stood up to brush off my jeans, I caught a glimpse of my reflection in the living room window. I looked pale, from overthinking things, most likely. *Get a grip,* I told myself. A man was working in our yard. He was interesting, thoughtful, pleasant to be with. I had made a point to show him respect. That was all.

After the promised tour of the yard, which turned out to be brief, Giles Owita and I agreed to let the azaleas bloom before discussing their fate again. Also, we planned to leave any notes for each other in the letter slot where he'd left his very first note to me. In parting, he promised to check his schedule regarding the pruning of my river birch.

But there was one more thing we needed to discuss, something that needed to be resolved. I turned to him. "Would you please call me Carol? Mrs. Wall sounds so formal."

"You would prefer that?"

"I would, truly. You can call me Carol, and I will call you Giles."

Giles smiled and looked past me, and in that moment I realized that he would never call me Carol, the same way he would never look me directly in the eye. The same way I would never strip myself naked and walk down the middle of our street. Such things just weren't done in our cultures. Still, I hoped to convince him one day.

"*Erokamano*, Giles," I said to him as we stood on the sidewalk in front of my house. "I have been practicing the pronunciation."

"*Wabironenore*, Mrs. Wall," he answered, and then turned to walk uphill to his car.

I went inside to my kitchen counter. I looked at the marble notebook and did my best to hold my breathing steady. From the windowsill, a small color photo of my sister Barbara smiled sweetly out at me. My nails were squeaky clean, but nonetheless I washed my hands, using a brush with stiff bristles to attack any grit or dirt that might have made its way into a crevice of my skin or underneath my nails.

I dried my hands on a clean paper towel and found a magic marker. *GARDEN NOTES*, I wrote on my marble notebook. I had much to learn from Giles, and I promised myself that I would write it all down so that I couldn't possibly forget.

MONDAY

Dear Giles,

I hope you and your family have had a good weekend. I hate to make this type of request again, but could you possibly arrange to come for pruning of the river birch at a time when I can be present? If my van is in the driveway, just ring the bell. Or, if you know ahead of time, leave me a note here, per our agreement. I'm a little unsure of the shape I want and the degree to which I should curb the growth of that particular tree, so I hope it's okay if I guide you in-progress. The librarian at school is helping me find a book on the subject, as I hesitate to approach Melanie or Sarah with requests for advice. As you know, it's their busy season. I neglected to tell you that, long ago and with a rare burst of gardening enthusiasm, I planted the river birch myself. It was just after we moved into the house, a time when the tree was barely taller than the children. But, like my children, it has grown quickly, taking to the skies more or less without my permission, though I'm glad to see its roots have apparently sunk in deep beside this creek, where it seems to thrive.

I must admit the azaleas look better already. Sarah and I strolled around to the side of the house yesterday afternoon, and we were able to see the tips of their pink buds showing through the leaves. You'll be glad to know that she encouraged me to listen to your advice, on all fronts, as you are "the best," as she put it.

My prayers for Lok continue. Please always let me know if there is any news. Thank you for all your efforts, and be sure to leave your bill, from time to time. I look forward to working with you again soon.

Sincerely,

Carol Wall

WEDNESDAY

Dear Mrs. Wall,

My calendar is clear on Friday. Bienta and I have some business matters to attend to in the a.m., but I will check by your house after your school hours and will bring the appropriate tools.

Lok's case appeared to be nearing a breakthrough recently, but last evening's phone call from Bienta's sister in Nairobi (it was after midnight there) brought news of yet more entanglements with medical examinations, affidavits, and other paperwork. After so long a time has passed, some of the materials lapse out of date, and the process must be started again, with more funds due *and waiting periods in effect. I am sorry to tell you that there can be corruption anywhere on the globe, and persons who are highly placed are often subject to temptation. A travel visa to the US is much coveted. Sometimes, even DNA tests are required to establish the applicant's identity. We are in the midst of that process.*

In any case, Bienta and I thank you for your prayers. She has always been very devout, and insists that, in any circumstance, prayers are needed even more than patience, more than funds, signatures, sworn statements, or anything whatsoever that a government run by human beings might be able to produce. As we "wait in joyful hope" for our daughter, I look forward to the pleasure of finding the best lines of your beautiful birch tree in among the overflourishing branches and copious leaves it has produced during the years of your children's growing up. That day of cutting back will produce a clearer shape that will bring its own rewards. I will submit my first bill after that.

In closing, let me say that I am going to bring an extra pair of gardening gloves on Friday. Oftentimes, assistance is needed with larger garden projects, and I was delighted to hear that you will be on hand to help.

With best wishes,

Giles Owita

5.

Anticipated Blooms

Agentle breeze sifted through the branches of my backyard birch tree. Giles stood beside me, managing to look both serious and cheerful. His left hand grasped a pruning saw and pruning shears. I held out a clothbound book.

"Betula nigra *is occasionally called a river birch*," I read aloud. "*The tree is native to an area spanning most parts of the eastern United States . . . from New Hampshire west to southern Minnesota, and south to northern Florida and West Texas. It often grows to eighty feet, with multiple trunks. After pruning, scaffold branches should look like ascending spokes around a central axle.*" I turned the book toward Giles, to show him the picture. He nodded respectfully, to indicate he took it in. "*This will provide a structurally strong tree that is attractive, balanced, and allows sunlight to penetrate and wind to pass through the canopy. To ensure strength, major scaffold branches should have at least eight inches and preferably twenty inches of vertical separation.* Should I get a yardstick, Giles? I have one in the house."

He didn't answer right away. I heard the whistling wind and birdsong, the flapping wings of a red hawk soaring high above the burbling creek. I wondered if Giles appreciated the information I was sharing with him. I hadn't meant to come across as arrogant or heavy-handed. It's just that, working together, I thought we could achieve the best result.

"This tree is a fine example of a popular type of birch that likes to get its feet wet," Giles finally answered. "I have pruned the species before, and will not need a yardstick."

"Don't let me interfere." I closed the landscaping book. Apparently, Giles saw this as his prompt to get down to business. He took two giant, backward steps, his face reflecting concentrated energy, and I realized with horror that he was planning to climb the tree. I called out to him, "Don't you need a ladder, Giles?"

He sprinted past me, a streak of energy advancing toward the tree. He pushed himself off with one foot, and as I watched him rise, I was amazed that a person of his age could be so nimble, strong, and fearless. The branches shuddered as he found a place within. His tennis shoes scraped the bark until they settled on the first of the substantial horizontal limbs, about six feet from the ground. From there, he climbed until he disappeared into the canopy of leaves. Aware that I had absolutely nothing to contribute to this endeavor, I retreated to the asphalt pad that made up our basketball court, and pulled out a black metal lawn chair to sit in. I couldn't see Giles, but I could hear him working and see the shaking of the leaves.

I set my book aside. My gaze fell on a brand-new pair of dark green garden gloves that Giles had taken from his pocket when he arrived (although I'd prayed he would forget). They lay on top of his folded gray sweatshirt, in the shadow of the birch tree, exactly where he had placed them with what seemed a careful glance in my direction.

A ripple of annoyance passed over me. He brought them, but then gave no explanation. I walked closer and confirmed my initial impression: two green cotton gloves that were bulky and too large for me. I studied them. My mouth went dry. I hoped he didn't intend for me to dig in the dirt. The very thought of it made me queasy. I could have simply asked Giles what he meant by needing my "assistance." But I sensed I'd pressed the limits by reading to him from the book.

The leaves that shielded Giles shivered. "Are you okay, Mrs. Wall?"

Rhudy tilted his snout up and barked to let me know that he was on the job. I scrambled back to get my book. "Are you about to make your cut?"

"I will await instruction," he said.

I pictured him hanging precariously by one arm, one foot propped against a sturdy limb and the pruning saw poised for action. I needed to hurry. "Here it says you don't cut flush against the tree when pruning," I called up to him.

"Okay."

"You're supposed to leave an angle, which I thought was interesting. I wish you could see this picture. It shows why you don't want it to be flat, because disease and weeping can result from the way it used to be done, in the old days. Flat against the limb, that is. We don't want that."

"Very good," Giles said. "It's very true."

I heard the sound of sawing and pictured sunlight flashing on the steely blade.

"Giles, how long have you been working with plants?" I was surprised to realize I hadn't asked him this before.

The sawing stopped.

"I have loved them ever since I can remember. Especially the flowers." His voice was soft, yet vibrant with feeling.

"Do you have the river birch in Kenya?"

"There have been cultivars from other lands. But they are not native."

I felt my cheeks grow red with embarrassment, and the tiniest suspicion that I had made a mistake in thinking that Giles needed my help in pruning the tree properly. I skipped to another page I'd marked. It showed a row of inkberry hollies intermingled with some rhododendron, planted in an interesting design at the base of a traditional brick house like ours. Azaleas played no role in the design.

Perhaps I just needed to modernize Giles's perspective on azaleas. I called up to him, "Don't you think certain plants go in and out of style?"

There was no reply, and I wondered if he'd heard me. Just as I was about to repeat myself, the pages of my landscaping book were ravaged by the wind. My fingers grasped the cover tightly so it wouldn't be blown away. The sheets whipped forward in quick succession, right to left, as if a nervous ghost were turning them. To gain control, I held the volume to my chest and planted my feet more firmly. Then my gaze fell again to the extra pair of garden gloves, whose lifeless fingers curved suggestively as if, like me, they'd heard a rumor of some unnamed task ahead and wanted to be prepared.

Giles's own gloves were a chestnut brown. He had produced them from the pocket of his navy work suit just before he leaped into the tree. Now, as I stood watching, one of Giles's gloves somersaulted past lime-green leaves with silver undersides that seemed alive. The glove tumbled quickly past the slender branches with their scrolling, vanilla-colored bark and the tawny, paper-like curls along the triple trunk. It landed among the blades of grass where our children used to have their summer picnics. I rushed to pick it up.

"Please stand back," Giles said, his voice unusually firm. I closed my garden book with a resonant snapping sound and scurried across the grass to the basketball court, where my metal lawn chair waited. Rhudy, too, backed off, as if he understood the warning. I heard more sawing, and the first branch landed some twelve or fifteen feet away from where I sat. It was about the length of a golf club, but thicker in diameter, with a smaller branch and fluttering leaves attached to make a lopsided V.

"Rhudy, can you see the sky?" Giles inquired, clearly pleased.

A triangle of bright blue showed through the airy space that Giles had just created. The lime-green splendor of the leaves was even more pronounced against the turquoise of the cloudless sky.

"That's absolutely beautiful," I said.

"Now this lovely tree can breathe," Giles said, with obvious pleasure.

"That goes for all of us." Only in that moment did I realize how coiled and ready I'd been for disaster, how truly uncertain I had been that Giles knew what he was doing and wouldn't come tumbling out of that tree like his work glove. I heard Giles sawing again, and another branch of similar size to the first rattled down. It cut a second elegant swath of blue near the top of the birch.

Then an answer came to me regarding the mystery of the dark green gloves. Giles probably wanted me to join him in picking up debris afterward. Relieved that no digging would be involved, I scooped a few small twigs from the ground and started a pile. A short while later, Giles landed on his feet with expert poise. I retreated to the kitchen to get him a bottle of water from the fridge. From this higher vantage point I gained a full perspective on the transformation of my tree. Where once there was merely a short white triple trunk with a shapeless expanse of green on top, I now saw leaves and branches; limbs that reached for the sky. A blue jay perching on one of the higher branches greeted me with his shiny eyes. A pair of crimson cardinals swooped in just below, as if to say, "Where have you been?" Giles's masterful pruning also yielded clearer glimpses of sunlight dancing on the churning creek. Against the backdrop of these improvements, I was surprised to notice Giles making quick work of the clean-up job that I thought was going to be mine. At the rate he was going, he'd be finished picking up debris and clearing the space before I could get out there. Dick had always chastised me for delaying workers around the house, keeping them talking when they were on the clock. It suddenly occurred to me that Giles was probably in a hurry and had a schedule to keep—visits to other yards, or maybe his shift at the grocery store. Not for the first time, it struck me how exhausted he must be. I grabbed my checkbook and headed out to the yard with the bottle of water.

There was a lightness in my step as I walked toward Giles, but my sense of joy was short-lived. As I handed him the bottle, he extended the dark green gloves to me.

"But, you've already cleaned up, and made quick work of it!" I protested. "The yard looks great."

"But there is one more thing we need to do," Giles said.

He picked up the shovel he'd propped against our fence and made a few preliminary stabs into the sparsely growing grass along a very empty, eight-foot area beside the pickets.

"What on earth are you doing, Giles?"

"We're going to make a flower bed," he said. His blade chopped away at the ground. "There is good news. I have some specimens found in another client's small greenhouse. She offered them to me, because she has so many things, and I told her, 'I know a very nice lady who may want them.' They are annuals, so if you don't like them, leave them in the ground and they will not come back next year. Their colors are deep red, with some blooms being purple, and another species, yellow. That wouldn't be too many colors, would it? I could bring them to your yard when the danger of frost has passed, in mid-May, installing them while you are at school, if you like, and you could just return home to the beauty. But for now, we should prepare the soil. It's why you need your gloves." The whole time Giles talked, he dug away at the ground with rhythmic cuts. Then he stopped, and in his inimitable way he looked at me without actually looking at me. Although his face was as still and unreadable as always, there was an unmistakable twinkle of amusement in his eyes. "Will you help me get it ready, Mrs. Wall? After all, it is your yard."

I desperately wanted to be able to twinkle back at him, a silent acknowledgment of our tug-of-war over the azaleas and my lecturing to him from the garden book that he so clearly didn't need. But instead, I struggled to maintain a pleasant expression. A familiar feeling of dread sank like a stone in my stomach— and in my heart. I turned around to face the creek, grasping the fence pickets until my knuckles turned white. I hoped that Giles wouldn't notice my distress at the mere thought of joining in with his project. It amazed me how he didn't seem troubled in the least by any sad thoughts of the way his blooms would inevitably turn brown in spite of his best efforts. I so wanted Giles to think well of me, and I wondered how I could possibly explain to him that what he loved so much filled me with horror. How could I tell him that I couldn't abide the feel of dirt beneath my fingernails, or even weighing heavily on a damp garden glove? He would think I was crazy if I confessed how repelled I was at the idea of a flower garden planted in the yard that collared our cozy house. I shuddered, imagining petals falling away in advance of the winter that was always on its way.

Instead of making my confession, I told myself that Giles was just a person working in my yard, or, at best, a casual friend who didn't need to hear my complicated family history.

"I don't like dirt around my fingernails," I said. "And gardening gloves make me feel clumsy. Is that so hard to understand?" I realized with embarrassment that despite my best intentions my voice had grown testy, with a sharp edge. But I couldn't stop myself once started. "This was a basketball court for my children. It's not a place for a garden."

Giles glanced around as if weighing our options. "I'll space the flowers out. The clusters will be beautiful, not overwhelming. The basketball stays in the garage these days, as far as I can tell. So our problem there is solved."

That marked the end my patience. "No, Giles!" I burst out. My voice was now angry. Then, as if to prove to both of us that I had no business employing anybody, I said, "We're willing to increase your pay." I truly was a ridiculous woman, I thought to myself—bribing my own gardener not to do his work.

Giles's face registered my panic and he trained his gaze on a point very near my face. It was the closest he had ever come to looking me in the eye. "Don't worry," he said, a little twinkle of humor returning to his face. "A riotous blend of flowers is not required." Then his expression grew brighter, as if an idea had just occurred to him. "We will plant some shrubs, though not azaleas."

I looked at Giles and then up through the canopy of what was now a well-pruned birch tree. I had not realized the extent to which the leafy tree had bathed our yard in shadow. Things looked more cheerful with the brighter light pouring in. Even Rhudy seemed delighted. He celebrated by running circles around the tree. Giles bent down to pet him.

"Rhudy, I see you are a gardener, too," he said, pointing to a hole Rhudy had managed to dig near the base of the tree while we were otherwise occupied. I thought about Giles's stubborn resistance on the subject of removing the azaleas last week, and his patience today while I was holding forth on the instructions for trimming the birch tree. At times, Giles seemed to meditate before taking action, but once a decision had been made, it didn't take him long to act. His intuition seemed to guide him in important matters.

As a senior in high school, I studied Aristotle's views on the nature of friendship. He described the highest level as "a friendship of virtue," where there was no agenda other than a devotion to the welfare of your friend. There was no place for selfishness in this kind of relationship. It was more like a calling, anchored in respect and a keen regard for the other person that could not easily be shaken. Was it possible that Giles Owita could be such a friend to me? Was I worthy of being *his* friend? There was only one way to find out.

Unspoken truth lay between us. I made a quick decision of my own.

"Some people say I have a gloomy outlook," I said. "I think they may have a point, but I want to tell you about something that makes me that way. Almost ten years ago, I had some tests that indicated breast cancer. I had a lumpectomy and a series of radiation treatments, and my prognosis is good. But the whole experience changed me spiritually and emotionally. I just can't stop worrying about it. Anytime I see the breast cancer commercials on TV, or I see well-adjusted women in their pink sweatshirts, I just cannot identify with them. I wonder what is going to happen to me next. I can't stand to think about losing all of the wonderful things in my life."

"Yes, Mrs. Wall. I understand." Giles looked across the creek and his eyes grew narrow. His expression, as always, was difficult to read. "Worry is a part of life. For now, there is work to do in our garden." He knelt to sift through the soil with his bare hands. The sight was mesmerizing.

Filled with a growing resolve, I put my naked hands inside the green garden gloves. My fingers felt bony, too small for the yawning openings. *Just touch the soil of Mother Earth. It would make Giles happy,* a voice inside me said. "All right, Giles. But I'd rather do it this way." I tugged the right glove off, and then the left.

I allowed my fingertips to brush the surface of the ground.

The soil felt frozen at first, yet I found my fingers soon exploring dirt that clumped and caked, and if dry, fell in ribbons from one hand to the other. Its color and texture reminded me of coffee grounds. I recalled how, in my Southern childhood, we would often go barefoot, without worrying about bee stings, broken glass, parasites, or jagged rocks. By August, our feet would be leather-tough, prepared for anything. The sound of bare feet slapping against dry, hard-packed dirt as we played our games of softball, kickball, tag, or red rover came back to me. It had been a long time since I thought of how quick I used to be—a cagey, confident teammate almost always chosen first when older kids were forming their teams.

As I pondered these memories, I was vaguely aware of Giles going back and forth to the garage for supplies. He handed me a familiar-looking garden claw with chipped red paint on the wooden handle, and I began to lose myself in the work that was nearly as old as the planet itself—scraping, digging, and mixing to prepare the soil for what it did best.

While I worked, I fell under the spell of other memories. The effect was hypnotic. Even my awareness of Giles faded as I was transported to a solitary hemlock where I used to stop for a rest as a child walking home from school. I hadn't thought of it in years. In my vision, I was sitting in the grass beside the compact tree with feathery-looking, dull blue branches stretching over me. There were bright yellow dandelions around the skirt of the cotton print dress my grandmother had sewn for me, and I was still young enough to feel sorry for children whose grandmothers didn't sew and, therefore, sadly, had to buy their dresses from the stodgy women's clothing stores downtown. I wasn't on a schedule and had no checklist for the day. All I knew was the happy hum of living in a household run efficiently and lovingly.

I remembered also how I skated down the steep-pitched hill of Sleepy Hollow Road with older children, at a breakneck pace. Or, as the sun began to set, how I climbed my yellow apple tree to the very top with a library book tucked under my arm. I played touch football with neighborhood boys and was a noted wide receiver (even *if* a girl) in our flat front yard whose curving limestone sidewalk formed the perfect undulating fifty-yard line. Breezes carried the delicious aroma of tender roast beef and buttered biscuits wafting out onto our football field from Mama's kitchen. She loved to watch our games, but at some point I realized that what she really wanted was another baby and another. She wanted happy, healthy children to fill every corner of her home, to make up for the losses she had suffered. Instead she had to settle for two, me and my younger sister, Judy.

Finally, with the ground prepared, I picked up the gloves and draped them on the fence. Giles and I stood together, looking out across the creek.

"Are your parents living, Giles?"

His eyes grew soft. "My father is deceased. But he had a very interesting and eventful life. His first wife was killed by lightning on Lake Victoria. This would have been in the early forties.

My mother, age twelve or thirteen at the time, was brought into the household as a babysitter to my father's motherless children. He was an herbalist, within our tribe. Very much older than my mother, who still lives. She was only fourteen when I was born. We are very close, and when I go there, we choose to spend much time talking, and can talk almost forever. She remembers everything. She likes to laugh."

"I can picture it easily, Giles."

"She is scarcely five feet tall, yet smart and resourceful," he continued. "It is said she delivered me as the sun was setting, and then took me out with her to do some chores. Many taller people on the island still look up to her."

"Did she have other children?"

"I have three sisters and one elder brother who live. Four brothers were lost in childhood. Their ailments seemed to be mysterious. I always thought it may have been a heart arrhythmia, but no one knew for sure. Out in the humid air playing with other children of the village, they simply collapsed, one when he was quite young, and the other, a few years later. I have worried about my own sons, fearing an inherited disorder. Oh, how my mother grieved. I remember her slumped over their lifeless bodies, wailing, unable to be consoled. They were wonderful, lively brothers and friends. I did not have time to say goodbye. We thought we had them, but as the islanders say, it seems they were merely visitors, after all. They 'went back.'"

"Went back? That's a beautiful phrase. It seems comforting, somehow. How long did it take your mother to get over that?"

"You never get over certain grief. But there is no pressure in my culture to get over losing a loved one. It is very different from here. Childhood is very dangerous where I come from. There are many perils and diseases. That is why we sometimes say that a child is not your own until he has survived measles."

My voice stuck somewhere in my throat. Suddenly, a brisk wind brought heavy raindrops, stinging our faces and peppering the fabric of our work clothes. Through all this, the sun continued to shine. Then the rain stopped just as quickly as it had begun.

"When was the last time you saw your mother?" I asked.

But before he could answer, we heard a car horn bleating from the street side of the house.

"Bienta!" he cried out, alarmed. "What time is it, Mrs. Wall?"

With an air of urgency, he gathered his things. I trailed him as he raced around the house, toward the street. The sky-blue Neon was parked at the curb, Bienta at the wheel. She reached over and moved a stack of newspapers from the passenger seat to the floor.

"Our other vehicle is under repair," Giles called back over his shoulder as he opened the passenger door. "We are sharing today."

He rolled the window down to offer me his goodbyes. Bienta spoke to him in a foreign language. I hoped she was asking him to introduce us.

I was pleased when he said, "Mrs. Wall, may I present Bienta, my wife? Bienta, please meet Mrs. Wall."

"Everyone calls me Carol," I offered, hoping this time it would stick.

Bienta extended her hand. Her features were pleasantly arranged on a pretty face and her lips shimmered with a hint of gloss. Like her husband, she looked to be a little over fifty. She was dressed in jeans and a red-knit, short-sleeved shirt. Her hair was very short and she wore gold hoop earrings.

"It's very nice to meet you, Bienta," I said.

She looked at me steadily. Brought up on the mainland and educated in private schools, Bienta apparently did not observe the rules about direct eye contact that Giles learned in his village. Then she spoke to Giles in Luo again.

"My wife is saying . . ." Giles began to translate.

Bienta interrupted him. "You sing in the choir at Saint Benedict's." She spoke with enthusiasm and a hint of a British accent. "I realize now that I have seen you, all along, going up for Communion with your fellow choir mates. Giles told me the names of a Mr. and Mrs. Wall and described where you live 'with your little beagle by the river,' as he is fond of pointing out. But I didn't know that it was you, a fellow parishioner whom I so easily would recognize by sight, not until I saw you come around the corner of your house, just now."

"You are a parishioner at Saint Benedict's, and have seen me?" I repeated, unable to hide my astonishment. I felt terribly embarrassed that I hadn't recognized her, and it must have showed.

"I often wear my tribal head wrap to Mass," Bienta said. "Perhaps that's why you didn't recognize me today. Don't feel bad.

Also, your group is already at the altar just as we are standing up to join the line. I like to sit beside the window of Saint Elizabeth of Hungary. Have you ever sat there, in that golden light? She's the saint who fed bread to the poor, in the thirteenth century. She and her husband were of royal birth, so he felt such actions were beneath them. When her husband came to accuse her, Our Lord changed the bread in her apron into roses. It was one of her saintly miracles. We all need our occasional miracles, don't we, Mrs. Wall?"

"Miracles. Yes. I'll definitely take a few."

I wondered if Bienta thought of Lok as she studied the window each week at Mass. And what of the roses, Lok's favorite flower? I would have loved to see the Owitas' yard. I imagined it covered with roses.

"The yellow roses are quite beautiful," Bienta said, as if she read my mind.

"They are," I said. I waited, hoping she would mention her daughter.

Instead, Bienta and Giles said goodbye to me and I watched as she steered the car along Mount Vernon Road, toward the intersection. Bienta was no longer a theory or an abstraction, but a real person who drove a Neon and joined in the Communion line along with me. From now on, I would make it a point to look for her, sitting faithfully by her favorite saint, as I looked down from my seat in the choir loft.

6.

Approaching Systems

As we moved into summer after that first spring, our valley suffered through a stretch of suffocating heat that lasted well into September. Rain was scarce, but it seemed that Giles didn't need rain. Our yard continued to thrive in his gifted hands.

Giles had added more clients to his list and there were times when I might go a week or more without seeing him. If he arrived while I wasn't at home, he usually left me a note in the mail slot, reporting on what he'd done. I sometimes paused, going out to the van, simply to turn around and take a good look at a home and yard I now felt proud of. Two large brown ceramic pots, chosen by Giles and Sarah, flanked the front door. They held a muted purple, trailing species of geranium, the first new flowers I had agreed to. Giles was ecstatic to have won this little victory. Although I hadn't admitted this to him, I saw he was right about bringing out the beauty "that already belongs to your compound." With my consent, Giles had also planted three ink-berry hollies we ordered through Sarah, for the space we tilled that day beside the backyard fence. The leaves were glossy, pleas-ing to the eye, with pinpoint, pure white flowers.

When the azaleas bloomed I had a change of heart and told Giles we would keep them "one more year, at least."

As we strolled past them one humid afternoon, he said, "Their roots are deep, and they belong here."

In just one season, Giles had transformed our yard. Wider mulch beds framed the front yard shrubbery. Our boxwoods gleamed. Our neighbors conveyed shocked approval as they peddled cautious compliments, saying things like, "Your yard looks nice. Your grass is spongier, it seems. That man who comes around—we've seen him up at Sarah's house, too. Say, isn't he that guy who sometimes works at Foodland? We've heard he's good with growing things. Does he ever sleep?"

As June yielded to July, more neighbors ventured down the street to snag Giles for a curbside consultation. I could always spot them by their timid steps, or the blighted leaf or limp-looking blossom they cradled in their hands. "What do you think might be wrong?" they shyly asked Giles. Some even offered folded bills, offering to pay for his step-by-step instructions. But he declined to charge them for a moment's conversation. One neighbor joked that his techniques should be patented.

The first time I heard a neighbor holding Dick and me out as models, I stifled a giggle. I could tell Dick was pleased, too. I noticed he used a jauntier step when mowing. He lingered in the process, boldly stepping off the limited dimensions of our yard and stabbing the mower extra times into the shadows underneath the shrubbery to make sure that even unseen blades were uniformly clipped. His legs moved with an energy once seen only in his headlong dash to the nearest driving range or putting green. By summer's end, he sported a darker tan than usual.

Meanwhile, I suddenly became a weather-data addict. Checking the online forecast for our area was a soothing daily ritual. I developed a fondness for the local TV weather guy, who wore a bad toupee but used sexy terms like "warm front," "Doppler radar," and "relative humidity." As August rolled around, I even bought a *Farmers' Almanac*, leafing through it in the drugstore checkout line as if I were devouring a steamy romance novel. It was cozy, thinking of the bigger picture of a weather zone and how so many people were united by approaching systems no one could control. It was the most kinship I'd felt with my fellow man in many years.

Each Sunday, I looked for Bienta at church. After Mass, I usually tried to catch up with her by speed-walking toward her customary exit beside the baptismal font, but she eluded me every time. Dick suggested that maybe if I lingered beneath her favorite window, I might find her. But I had a feeling that I would never catch up with her, until and unless she wanted to be caught. I tried not dwelling on it but I couldn't help worrying that I'd done something to offend her, and it wasn't in my nature not to worry over things.

A typical summer Sunday also included a drive from church to Heathwood Hearth—to honor my father and my mother. When I arrived for our weekly ice cream date, they were always waiting eagerly in the velvety-green parlor. I helped them up into Dick's smaller four-door, and we drove through town looking at people's yards.

To make conversation and to try to keep Daddy tethered to the moment, I'd sometimes ask him questions to jog his memory. "Remember how you used to write that newspaper column, Daddy, featuring prominent citizens of Radford?" (He said no.) "Remember how we used to measure snowfall with the handle of a broomstick, every winter?" ("Yes," he answered. "I went sledding, and a little girl rode on my back.")

At times like that a flush made its way up my mother's cheeks. Though she might try to be stoic, her pale, freckled skin gave her away every time. I knew she wouldn't cry—Mama rarely caved in to sentiment. She'd had a lot of practice, I supposed. Meanwhile, I struggled to hold back tears. It had never once occurred to me to ask Mama to try feeling her feelings instead of just passing them on to me as in a game of hot potato. I blotted a tear that spilled onto my cheek and streaked down the side of my face.

Daddy occasionally seemed to be on the verge of knowing things that he'd forgotten. I tried to reconcile the reflection of the stranger in my rearview mirror with the father I knew, the man who ministered to the struggling from behind the cash register in his old hotel. Often he made small loans of money to the really hard up, knowing full well that they would never be paid back. Now he sat in the backseat of our car, fiddling with the child locks, gritting his teeth between heavy slurps of butter brickle ice cream and working on a theory of how it came to pass that I was driving him around.

On another Sunday afternoon, I drove my parents and their ice cream by my house when Giles was working in the yard. I called Giles over to the car to meet them and Daddy even managed to look a little pleasant, as if Giles were a regular at his hotel's newsstand, purchasing a stack of magazines, some paperbacks, and a copy of *The Wall Street Journal*. My mother's eyelids fluttered with evolving interest and approval as her gaze swept across the yard. She complimented Giles on his work. "My daughter speaks of you with high regard, and now I'm seeing why."

It was the first time in many weeks that I'd seen her pursue a pleasant conversation with anyone. This was a positive development. But, on the minus side, her gait had begun to get wobblier and she had stumbled several times. I had made an appointment with her doctor, but it was still weeks away.

I shared my concerns with Giles one day after he and my parents had met. He mentioned that she might want to start using a cane. Then a few days later, he surprised me by bringing one from home, for me to give to my mother. It was carved from one piece of wood with figures of zebras, elephants, giraffes, and other exotic animals springing to life on the handle. Giles told me that among Luos, each elder selected the style of his cane. The more intricate the cane, the higher the status of the elder in the community. This cane's wood was from the Nile tulip tree.

I fingered the curve of the cane. "So wonderful," I said, marveling over the animals that circled the handle with such liveliness. I thought how miraculous it would be if the animals' graceful movements could be transferred to whoever used it. Once again, my English teacher's knack for fantasy swept me off my feet and I shook myself back to reality.

"We can't accept this lovely cane, Giles! It's a work of art."

"It is okay," Giles answered me indulgently, as if speaking to a child. "Consider it a loan, and I will take it back someday. Better that it be used by a person of spiritual depth and upright character, someone exactly like your mother. I felt her kindness and her suffering as we spoke that day at your compound."

"Did you, Giles?" I think I was even more grateful for his regard for my mother than I was for the generous loan of the cane.

I remembered hesitating as Giles held the cane toward me. Something in the transfer seemed ill-advised, though I had no words to explain the odd sensation, and it became another mystery I associated with him. There would come a time when I thought back on that moment as a foreshadowing. Were our future troubles lurking, even then? Or had I placed them there, in hindsight?

7.

The Canopy of the
Yukon Gold Potato

B y the end of that first transformational summer with Giles, I found myself more outwardly directed. It was a pleasant break from the usual for me. Instead of dithering in the house, checking for lumps and bumps and potential killer moles each time I passed a mirror, I was content to sit on my front porch and watch the children play across the street. Any problems waiting for me in the future seemed remote.

One September afternoon, the sky a bottomless shade of blue that I always associated with the arrival of autumn, I made my way to the Garden Shoppe. Sarah had called me about a just-delivered special order of pumpkins. She offered to set a few aside for me. Before we hung up, Sarah and I shared a laugh, agreeing that the upper-crust ladies in town would pay a hundred dollars a pumpkin, just to get what they wanted.

"And *two* hundred dollars to get what *you* want!" Sarah added.

When I arrived, I scanned the shop, greenhouse, and surrounding parking lot for Giles, but there was no sign of him. I was secretly relieved. I'd been hoping to have a moment alone with Sarah to ask her about Giles's somewhat cavalier attitude toward the lists I gave him. In the end, his ideas were always superior to my instructions, but still, there were times I just wanted him to do things my way, without question.

As I neared the middle greenhouse, the door sprung open and Sarah hurried toward me, wagon in tow. She seemed full of energy. "Hi, stranger," she called out. She clutched a pair of deep blue gardening gloves with a stamped-on ladybug design, a sample from the greenhouse inventory. "Can I interest you in some pumpkins?"

"I really appreciate this," I said, kneeling to inspect them. "Did you actually hide these for me?"

"Sort of. I left a few up front. Melanie wants a big display near the entrance."

Sarah's face was flushed. So much of her work was physical, and I couldn't help envying her vigor. Whenever I stopped by, she was most often toting people's heavy purchases on her wagon: pots of shrubs, crocks, and birdbaths.

I selected some beautiful pumpkins, more than the three I had planned. We pulled up to a spot just inside the greenhouse door and marked my haul "Sold" so we'd be free to take a stroll.

At this point, I recalled that I needed to get some mums.

"Giles pulled out the geraniums last week, the ones in those crocks by the door. I guess you saw."

"Yes. They were gorgeous at their peak," Sarah said.

"I've been meaning to tell you, Sarah, Giles is absolutely wonderful. I can't thank you enough for recommending him."

"Isn't he amazing? Henry and I love him, too. And Melanie adores him."

"I have something to ask you, Sarah. Something sort of confidential, and if you feel you can't answer, I'll completely understand."

"For heaven's sake, Carol. What is it?"

"Do you actually give Giles a work list around here? And if so, does he follow it?"

Sarah stopped and set a fist against her hip. I paused, mid-step.

"Are you still miffed about your azaleas, Carol?"

"Well, not 'miffed,' but I . . ."

She gave a small chuckle. "When Giles is working in a retail setting, it's totally different. He has no cause to go off-script, because no roots have been put down, and everything is up for sale. But when he works in my yard, I do have to watch him." She lowered her voice before continuing. "He doesn't like to take things out unless he's found a home for them. At first, I thought it was really strange. It kind of made me mad because it seemed like he was being stubborn. But it has also made me think twice about a few things, myself. Is it right to tear out specimens because we're bored with them, even when we know that some TLC will bring them back around? Please don't tell Melanie I said this. It's hardly good for business. I'm not going to say this to another soul. But, you know, maybe it makes me a better person to accept what I have, and not always feel like the perfect yard is just out of reach."

"I think I know what you mean. Once, Giles offered to bring me some flowers from a lady who had an overstuffed greenhouse. I think I might have hurt his feelings by declining the offer."

"Recycling. That's his policy. He can't imagine no one wants them," Sarah said.

"I never thought of it that way. 'Recycling.' That makes us modern. Ethical. Responsible Keepers of the Planet. I like the sound of it."

Sarah picked out some yellow mums for me to use on the front porch. We each carried a pot as we walked toward the third greenhouse, which housed the cash register. Sarah kept talking a steady stream. "Melanie was saying just last week that if we had a full-time opening for a horticulture specialist, with decent benefits and so forth, we would offer it to Giles."

"You would?"

"Absolutely. In a heartbeat. But why do you look so surprised?"

"Oh, I'm not surprised at all. I'm just happy to hear that you admire him as much as I do. I just think it's amazing what he's learned over the years, working in people's yards."

Any further words stuck in my throat because of the look of shock on Sarah's face. "Carol, didn't I tell you about Giles's background?"

"What are you talking about?" The tenor of my voice spiked uncomfortably, and I had the horrible sensation that I'd gotten something terribly wrong. Sarah asked me to wait a moment, and told me she'd be right back. Standing there, alone and braced against my racing thoughts, I felt off-balance.

Sarah returned, slightly out of breath and holding a piece of paper. "Here. I printed it out. His application. Read it, Carol, and you'll see that he could talk a million years and not convey the half of what he knows. He's gifted, yes, but this comes down to plain hard work and academic prowess. He wrote a very technical dissertation about the canopy of the Yukon Gold potato. He's done many projects in the field. What on earth have you been thinking, crazy girl? Where have you been?"

I took the paper from her hand. I skimmed the list of academic honors, college teaching, working for the government in horticultural and agricultural research in Kenya, and lastly, attaining his doctor of philosophy in horticulture from Virginia Tech, where I had spent my first two years of college before Dick and I were married, some thirty-five miles removed from where I stood, disgraced, in the here and now. The school was known internationally for its programs in horticulture. In fact, its horticulture students were the pride and joy of the university.

I finished reading and remained silent for a moment. I remembered that day when I read to him from the gardening

guide, and quizzed him on his familiarity with pruning that particular species of tree. Somehow I'd known that day of the tree
pruning that I was making a mistake. I'd felt it creeping up on
me, but I'd ignored the little voice inside telling me to watch
out. What a fool Giles must have thought I was. *Lord, Carol,* I
thought to myself, *you've gone and done it again.*

It was like a near-death experience, the way scenes of my
various social embarrassments flashed before my eyes. Prior to
this, the worst of my faux pas had occurred early in my marriage
to Dick, when he was a young lawyer. His senior partner's wife,
Dorothy, was a prominent member of local society and she invited me to be a docent for the house tour that she was hosting.
She stationed me in her bedroom, and I was supposed to explain
the origins of the various furnishings. The one thing she hadn't
told me about, though, was the portrait that sat on a table by her
bed. The woman in the painting had tightly permed hair, but
otherwise she looked exactly like Dorothy's husband, John. *She
must be John's mother,* I thought to myself. Once the tour was over,
the docents and our hostess all gathered. An introvert by nature,
I was often socially awkward, plus I was a good thirty years
younger than she and already feeling like a fish out of water. In
a doomed attempt to make conversation, I said, "Dorothy, that
is such a good painting in your bedroom, and it looks so much
like John that it's just got to be his mother."

The seconds that followed were like the electricity-filled moments before a lightning strike, when you know something bad

is about to happen. And then it hit me. The "woman" in that painting was John himself, during an ill-advised flirtation with a perm. In my defense, he looked ridiculous, with hair so tall and stiff it was like a bouffant. But there's no defending what I did next. In a rush of fear-induced adrenaline, I said, "Well, that painting sure needs a haircut."

I went home and stayed in bed for a good several days after that. But even that mortification was nowhere near what I felt now, recalling just how condescending I'd been to Giles.

"Not once did I ever suspect or venture to ask about his education," I finally managed to say to Sarah.

"I'm so sorry, Carol, I just assumed you knew. He and Bienta came to the States fourteen years ago, in large part so they could both go to graduate school here. Bienta has her own Ph.D., in human nutrition. Neither of them has been able to find jobs in their fields, though. That's why Bienta is nursing. I feel so badly for them. The whole reason they left their daughter behind in Kenya was so they could build a big new life here, and it just hasn't worked out for them. Their boys were both born here, though, so that's one blessing. And Giles just keeps working in that uncomplaining way of his. If we bring up anything even vaguely personal, we've noticed he'll soon find a chore that takes him to the far side of the property."

I put my head in my hands, just shaking my head.

"Oh, Carol," Sarah said. "You worry too much. Giles doesn't care about things like that. He's not looking to impress anyone.

I've seen the two of you chatting in your yard. He seems so relaxed, and his smile is broad and genuine. It's more than the stylized, reflexive smile he tends to give out in other settings. It's so rare what you have, as if you and Giles reached out across the Atlantic Ocean and whatever other barriers might exist between you and simply said, 'Let's be open. Life is short. Let's be friends.' Sometimes, as I'm driving by your house, I catch a glimpse of the two of you standing on the porch. I'll bet you haven't noticed, you're so engrossed in what you're talking about. It lifts my spirits whenever I see you like that. If I'm in a bad mood, I start feeling better, on the spot."

I thought back to the twinkle in Giles's eyes. I hoped Sarah was right, and that even though I'd acted like a goof and a dummy, he was more amused than offended. "Well, I'm going to begin by apologizing to Giles. I should have been addressing him as 'Doctor Owita' all along."

"For Lord's sake, Carol," Sarah said. "Giles respects you. He would never think . . ." She snatched her sunglasses off her head and stabbed the air for emphasis. "Don't you see that your courtesies are a two-way street? Don't you consider him a good judge of character? He knows you better than you think."

"We should be addressing him as 'Doctor,'" I said again. I couldn't get this omission off my mind.

Sarah shrugged. "He told us not to call him that, right at the get-go. And, listen. Does it really make a difference, in your friendship or your yard?"

I wondered. Would it have made a difference? Would I have

acted differently toward Giles at any point along the way if I had known?

Honest answer: Absolutely yes.

Reading to him from a book, indeed!

Instructing him on how to prune a river birch, for heaven's sake.

I got on my high horse and tried to teach him things. And he met my foolish efforts with humility.

"What's he doing working in my yard?" I managed to say. "He's spent his whole life preparing for something better."

"I think jobs in his field are hard to come by. A friend told Melanie that Giles gets interviews, but in the end, he never seems to get the job. Maybe it's his accent. I've also wondered if the way he looks away from people might be misinterpreted."

I pictured a committee of people assuming they could judge a man like Giles through formal conversation over herbal tea or lattes. What they really needed to witness was the way he led by example. I'd learned more about plants from him in just a few months than I ever could have learned from that gardening guide—or any other book, I imagined.

"All this time, I thought myself the academic. Isn't that pathetic, Sarah? Wait. Don't answer that. He's far surpassed us all. Let's simply leave it there." And with that, I gave her a sad smile and drove away.

When I got home, I pulled out my marble notebook. Like an ill-behaved student called to the principal's office, I sat at the kitchen table, turned to a clean page, and began to write.

1. Is the willingness to do manual labor incompatible with holding an advanced degree?
2. And DO YOU NOT REMEMBER how the "farmer's field" in Blacksburg was used to showcase the work of the school's top-flight aggie and horticulture students?
3. Were there stereotypes at play? Dick and I are baby boomers, after all. We are supposed to be enlightened!
4. Letter of apology:

Dearest Giles (Dr. Owita, I have learned):

I'm sorry. Even if I knew how to say those words in Luo, Swahili, and all the tribal languages of Kenya, it wouldn't be enough.

A friend has told me that you want to be a college professor. Until the day you get that job, I'd like to be your unofficial student. Here's what I've learned from you already:

—that intuition is a subset of intelligence (or maybe it's the other way)

—to count all persons as your equal and never make assumptions

—to nurture from a place within your soul

Signed: Your Very Humble Student on Mount Vernon Road

I ripped out the letter, folded the paper twice, and put it in a business envelope addressed to *Dr. Giles Owita.* Out of habit, I started to put the envelope in the letter slot, but something stopped me. It wasn't fitting that Giles should have to fish my apology out of the mail slot this time.

The next day, I saw the mailman walking up Mount Vernon. He had already passed our house and our regular mail was in the box. Quickly, I found a stamp and wrote out Giles's address, which I had fortuitously recorded on the inside cover of my notebook.

I opened the door.

"Charlie," I called out.

The young mailman looked back at me. I held up the envelope.

"I want to mail this in the proper, dignified way that befits a friend's accomplishments. Know what I mean?"

He removed his cap and scratched the top of his head. "Oh. All right. We can take care of that."

After taking my letter, he continued walking up Mount Vernon. I felt that I'd made a wise decision. From now on, I was going to hold myself to certain standards.

Three days later, I was surprised to find the corner of my own envelope protruding from the little mail slot to the left side of my door. I pulled it through. Giles had marked his name out with a heavy line, replacing it with: *Mrs. Carol Wall.*

My hands shook. I tore open the letter and read:

Dear Mrs. Wall,

Thank you for your note. You honor me by giving me the opportunity to tend your yard. No titles are needed. Next spring,

I believe we need to plant more hostas on the riverbank. Also, I am going to mix some chemicals to treat the spruces, with their stubborn spider mites. Your neighbor, Mr. Robert Maxim, has requested a consultation on his backyard problem. I will call on him next week, as soon as I complete some work on behalf of our grounds committee at Saint Benedict's. I am helping with the construction and design of the new koi pond, in memory of the children of our parishioners who have "gone back." Though this volunteer work on the committee's Memorial Pond will take much of my free time, please remember there is always a spot reserved for your yard on my schedule. I will await your call. As always, I am available to install more flowers in your yard.

I celebrate your listening ear and understanding heart.

Sincere regards,

Your friend ("osiepa," which means " friend" in my part of the world),

Giles Owita

8.

Every Yard Must Have Its Flowers

A few days later Sarah e-mailed me the first six pages of Giles's dissertation. It was a scientific tract about potato canopies with lots of graphs and charts. There was no poetic swooning over flowers. I felt more embarrassed than ever.

I started avoiding Giles, telling myself that I was giving him space to complete the memorial pond that he'd agreed to design for our church. I immersed myself in schoolwork and taking care of my parents.

But the interlude didn't last long. One late afternoon about a week later, I pulled my living room curtain back in time to see my "professor's" Neon cruising past. Intrigued, I opened my front door only a crack, peering out. Giles parked at the curb in front of Sarah's. He pulled some tools from the trunk and disappeared around the far side of her house, toward the entrance to the meditation garden. Dick wasn't due home for several hours because of a late appointment, so it was an open-ended evening, with takeout waiting on the kitchen counter in a bag. I heard our furnace kick on for the first time this season. Just the sound gave me a cozy, nesting feeling.

It looked like no one was home at Sarah's house. Her porch light was on. A brief chat with Giles would fit perfectly into this lonely corner of my day. Afterward, we could both reclaim our dignity and I could pretend that my terrible faux pas had never happened. I pulled on a hooded jacket.

I walked to Sarah's, pausing in her front yard. Her house was the largest and most elegant in the neighborhood, with a charming garden gate on each side of the lot. The entrance closest to us had a delicate trellis where the climbing roses had established themselves and appeared to be doing well. It was the first time I'd been in Sarah's backyard in quite a while, and I felt how the garden seemed to have a soul of its own. On this autumn evening, spotlights illuminated the ghostly forms of primrose and gardenias, mulberry-colored autumn sedum, orange and yellow daylilies, and coneflowers, with their petals pointed downward, set on wiry-looking stems. A quarter moon darted in and out of the clouds.

Giles was working at the far end of the lot, near the creek, and I called to him. "Doctor Owita."

"Mrs. Wall. It is you!" Giles said. He sounded genuinely happy to see me, and relief washed over me. I had made so many missteps on my way to being friends with Giles, yet I knew in this moment, and without asking, that Giles forgave me. "I should have been addressing you as doctor, all along," I quietly insisted. "You didn't tell me, Giles. I feel so bad about it. I hope you didn't think I was being disrespectful. Why, in Rusinga, they would have voted me off the island!"

His laugh was rich and sincere, and it ended with a sympathetic clucking sound that I'd grown to associate with him. Oh, how I had missed that million-dollar smile. More than I realized. "Should such a small thing matter, Mrs. Wall?"

I had planned to make a little speech, in penance. I was going to mention how I'd read to him about the river birch, citing how arrogant I had been and how I made assumptions based on biases. But the words evaporated in the cool night air. My explanation would have taken a long time, and even in a picture-perfect yard like this, there was much to do. I fleetingly wondered if Giles had brought an extra pair of gloves. *I shouldn't stay,* I told myself. But Giles didn't seem in a hurry. He leaned his rake on the back of one of the two wrought-iron benches, which were situated opposite each other, near the gate to the creek.

"I have been working on the children's memorial pond today, at church," he told me as I took a seat opposite where he stood. "The plaque has just been installed. It reads, 'For the children of Saint Benedict's who have flown from our arms to the arms of God.'"

"That's beautiful," I said. "We gave a contribution. In memory of someone. Have the fish been added, yet?"

"No koi. Not yet. We are still adjusting the various elements of this new ecosystem that will symbolize so much for grieving parents. It cannot be a casual matter, balancing this system and keeping the fish alive." Giles began to pace. He raised his eyebrows, and his expression grew brighter still as he explained that an overgrowth of algae blocking the sun was the reason that the pond was not doing well yet. "Right away, I saw the need for things like cattails and some ornamental grasses to deprive the algae of sunlight. I will drive to Blacksburg to get the water hyacinths and cattails, at the greenhouse. My wife and I will pay for them, if necessary, though I know the cost will not be much compared to all the good that will be gained."

"I'm so happy that you're doing this," I said. "There are many who have suffered for years over the death of a child. This will be a chance for those parents to honor their children, and to show how they're always remembered."

"This is what I said at the first committee meeting. I think they may have wished me to stay on topics relating to pond environments. Some of them had heard about Lake Victoria and knew that it is called 'the Sickly Giant,' due to algae forming and blocking the light. When I began to talk, I chose instead to speak to the committee as a father, trying to imagine the pain that loss of a child might bring."

"Giles, for some reason, we find that difficult to speak about in our culture."

"Mrs. Wall, your kind listening ear has given me the courage to voice my opinions. I have been noticing this more and more.

And that is very freeing. I'm humbled when I think of parents who have truly lost their children. If Lok is lost to us, it is just for a short while. And I have no one to blame but myself."

"Oh, Giles. I'm sure that's not true. You were trying to do what was best for your family when you left Kenya."

He looked to the sky once again. "I am to blame for leaving my daughter behind, in pursuit of the advanced degree. This doctorate. Yet we felt we could do much more for her by obtaining these credentials and securing teaching jobs in a university setting. I should have reminded myself that things do not always go as planned. My daughter pleaded to remain in Kenya to finish school among her many cousins and her friends. Bienta's mother was Lok's advocate in this, and my wife and I succumbed. We shouldn't have. In the years since we came over, travel has become more complicated. Now our precious daughter waits for us to be successful in our efforts. She must feel abandoned, though she doesn't say. Our lives are full of very many complications." Giles looked away. I had never seen him like this—he seemed forlorn.

"Lok was tiny when Bienta had her," Giles continued. "We knew a struggle lay ahead. She had arrived two months before her time. Fortunately, there was an incubator. It was the only one for many, many miles around, and our delightful, tiny Lok was placed in it at once!"

"Oh, my God," I said aloud, imagining a place where one couldn't take an incubator for granted.

"She was a fighter. Yes, she was!" he said. "We saw this right from the beginning. I held Bienta's hand each time we gazed on her. We had lost another baby, earlier, and so our hurting hearts were filled with love and longing for this tiny creature with her strong will and her tranquil face and tiny, pumping fists. We prayed so very, very hard that she would simply grow to live among us. Yet with every visit to the hospital, we saw her struggling. We feared that in spite of her tiny fists raised up, our prayers, and all our love, in the end she might *go back*."

"Oh, Giles. That must have been so hard. But Lok's not 'going back.' She's healthy now, and all these complications are the kind that can be dealt with. She will use the innate strength you describe, to get through this trial."

The cold was much more penetrating than I thought it would be, and I put my hood up. Giles looked at me expectantly. We always shared stories, back and forth. He had given me his, and now it was my turn to give him mine. I took a deep breath. The time had come for me to tell Giles about Barbara.

"Giles, I need to tell you something. It's something only Dick knows. Something I think about often, but can hardly ever bring myself to speak of."

Giles's off-center glance reflected his curiosity.

"My sister Barbara was born in 1950, a little more than a year before me. She was a Down syndrome baby. She died of heart failure ten days before her second birthday, when I was seven months old. It was Mother's Day, a Sunday. I don't remember this, of course. What I know is what my parents have told me over the years. The doctor who delivered Barbara was deliberately cruel. Apparently, he believed he was sparing my parents from forming an attachment to a child who couldn't possibly survive. He came into my mother's hospital room and announced to my parents that their baby girl was 'a Mongolian idiot,' and would 'never amount to anything.' They should put her in an institution and forget her, he advised. Instead, they took her home to the lovely nursery they had prepared, and a few weeks later, with high hopes in their hearts, they went to New York City, to see a specialist recommended by an army buddy and his wife who had settled there after the war. Barbara's case was one of the milder ones, the doctor said, in the kindest and most tactful way. But heart surgery was not an option and she would not live long. My advice to you, the doctor said, is to have another baby."

I paused. My hands trembled. I pushed my hood back, as if I'd been on the run for years and was finally ready to surrender. A gentle breeze moved through the roses. "I am the next chapter of our family story, Giles. And guilt weighs me down every day of my life. Every day I ask myself why Barbara had to die. I would have helped her had she lived. She could have counted on me. But I didn't get the chance to tell her."

Giles looked at me with sympathy. His heart had been tested, too. My tears began, but I found that I wasn't ashamed of them. I wiped my face on the sleeve of my jacket. I looked up to find Giles staring fiercely into the distance.

Stabbing the air with his pointer finger for emphasis, he said, "Your sister was an Innocent. A gift from life. Such children are incapable of guile. They bring out the best in us. The highest reaches of the heavens are reserved for them. The day your Barbara went back home, the angels welcomed her. Our Swahili word for angel is *malaika*. They rejoiced when your sister came back to them. She is one of them now."

"My father framed a poem about roses climbing a wall to the other side. That's how he thought of my sister."

"The poem brought you comfort, Mrs. Wall?"

"No. It didn't. I thought it was sad. But I pretended for him. Flowers have always depressed me, Giles. They just make me think of my sister's coffin. And how everything dies."

Giles hesitated, careful about his words as always. "Every yard must have its flowers, Mrs. Wall. Did you know there are flowers that bloom at night? For example, Dutchman's pipe cactus, dragon fruit flowers, four-o'clocks, and night gladiolus. Why not let new thoughts of all these flowers honor and console your baby sister at night, as you sleep? When you wake, go on with your happy, productive life, in which your own growing sense of joy should surely occupy an important spot and in which brightly colored blooms are not required.

"Flowers take many shapes, and there are many hues. The soil beneath our plodding feet is home to treasures as well as to many sorrows. This is very powerful, Mrs. Wall. Some may say, 'Move on,' but it is not so easy, is it? Sorrow follows us. The child in us is always there."

"Thank you, Giles, for listening. You're a good friend."

Giles and I kept each other company in silence a little while longer. Then I waited with him while he gathered up his tools, and walked with him to his car. My walk home from there was short, and the scent of Giles's flowers followed me all the way.

THE ROSE BEYOND THE WALL

A POEM BY A. L. FRINK

Near shady wall a rose once grew,

Budded and blossomed in God's free light,

Watered and fed by the morning dew,

Shedding its sweetness day and night.

As it grew and blossomed fair and tall,

Slowly rising to loftier height,

It came to a crevice in the wall

Through which there shone a beam of light.

Onward it crept with added strength

With never a thought of fear or pride.

It followed the light through the crevice's length

And unfolded itself on the other side.

Shall claim of death cause us to grieve

And make our courage faint and fall?

Nay! Let us faith and hope receive—

The rose still grows beyond the wall.

Scattering fragrance far and wide

Just as it did in days of yore,

Just as it did on the other side,

Just as it will forevermore.

Barbara Ann Gregory. Born: May 21, 1950

Entered Life Eternal: May 11, 1952

9.

Shades of White

Gradually, over the coming months, Giles broke me—cured me—of my dread of flowers.

The first stage of my treatment came in the spring, almost exactly a year after he first walked into our yard. It was an early April morning, and the freakish snow we'd had the night before had already melted.

In my walk-in closet, I took careful sips of my coffee. Deciding what to wear to school this time of year was tricky. I whisked through skirts and slacks and blouses on their hangers. Nothing appealed to me. It was Friday, and it flashed through my mind to simply conjure up a case of sniffles, call in sick, and climb beneath the covers with my mug of coffee, a couple of good books, and remote control in hand.

Instead, I pulled the curtain back to check the weather. This was when I saw the first of them, a nodding cluster of pure white daffodils between the first boxwood and the second, in the bed below my window.

I hadn't planned for these flowers. Yet at once, I knew whose loving hands had prepared this surprise.

My feet were bare, but I didn't let that stop me. With silky bathrobe fluttering, I ran down the stairs and flung open the front door.

"What are you doing?" Dick called out, but I kept going.

I stepped quickly through the yard. In the front, I found crocuses. They were tiny, white, and blooming in profusion. How long had they been there? How could I not have noticed them before?

In the backyard were more flowers—daffodils and crocuses. They were all in shades of white. They were everywhere, white flowers collaring the asphalt basketball court, and yet more white flowers spilling all along the fence line. There were white snowdrops and a stand of what I'd learn later was white alyssum. There would soon be white tulips and blossoms of sweet woodruff that I would come to love as well.

Stepping back to stand beneath the river birch, I knew that spring had come and, with it, an important moment in my history with Giles. *Every yard must have its flowers,* he'd said to me. How long ago must he have planned this surprise for me? It had to have been before I'd told him about Barbara. And yet somehow he knew that this sea of white flowers was what my broken heart needed.

With childlike joy, I reached to pluck a single daffodil. The scent was sweet. I wanted to see it standing upright in a small amount of water. Somewhere in this house of mine, though in another life, perhaps, I was pretty sure I had a bud vase.

During the summer months following my spring surprise, I found myself actually considering adding some color to our tidy green space. Those white flowers had been the tipping point, and now the slide into color seemed like a gentle, inevitable slope. Besides, I trusted Giles. So one late August afternoon, I asked him if he still had any colorful flowers needing a home. He was ecstatic.

"Nothing gaudy, Giles," I nervously reminded him. "And only a few, remember. Not too many and not too much color. It's really a form of recycling, when you think of it," I added piously.

My answer came in a matter of days when sweet red prim-roses appeared. They were quickly followed by some lemon-yellow daylilies to complement the dwarf-sized junipers that seemed a little lonely in their semicircular beds at the end of the sidewalk.

In early September, Giles brought purple-bearded irises for an empty-looking spot beside the driveway. Later that same day, I watched him work a corner of the backyard to make room for transplants taken from a larger hosta he had found "within a compound that was very, very crowded."

I would have loved to see what "very, very crowded" meant to him. Yet again, I wondered what his own yard looked like. Did he have a birch tree? Boxwoods? An arbor to accommodate a climbing rose? I thought of Lok, just as I did each time I saw a rose or when a silver jet passed overhead.

I thought of my own father. He no longer seemed to recognize me, and outings became increasingly difficult to manage. I was glad he hadn't been with me today, to see what I allowed to happen to Mama in Dr. Mitchell's parking lot.

Arriving at the doctor's office, I had felt noble helping Mama step out of my van. I imagined people smiling at the sight of us, saying, "Would you just look at that responsible, care-giving daughter? She is so devoted." Mama indeed looked well taken care of in a new navy sweat suit with white trim and a long, wide zipper on the jacket. Her hair had been freshly washed and trimmed at the Hearth's beauty shop. A new, off-white rinse with muted rosy tones brought out the best in her coloring, and as usual, her makeup was applied meticulously by her capable hand. Her running-style shoes were ones she hadn't worn much, and when I saw them as I was picking her up at the Hearth, I pushed down the impulse to suggest we go back inside and choose a pair she had already broken in a bit more, for safety's sake.

She insisted the new shoes were comfortable, and told me what I knew was a lie, saying that she'd been practicing walking in them for several weeks. "Carol, I am not going to fall. You worry too much.

"Aren't they bright and white?" she added as she took my arm. "They look new. As if I've been polishing them. Or saving them for the senior Olympics."

As we made our way across the parking lot toward Dr. Mitchell's office, I noticed Mama wincing with almost every step. I handed her a nondescript cane I had bought for her at Walmart. At first, she had mentioned bringing the Kenyan cane, which she was so proud of and intrigued by. I told her that I didn't think it was a good idea. The cane was too beautiful to use. Anyway, I had estimated that with only ten or twelve steps, we could reach the door of the doctor's office.

We began our journey. I had my lightweight Vera Bradley pocketbook on one arm, and my mother's Aigner bag dangled from my other shoulder. Every woman knows that when you control someone's pocketbook, you are the Alpha Girl. My mother was using her cane with one hand and holding on to my elbow with the other. She was safe and I was in charge. Or, that's what I thought.

But when we reached the step-up for the curb, it seemed I had her in my sights one moment, and then, before I knew it, she had fallen hard. With her arms so weak and reflexes slow, she had no means of breaking her fall. I watched helplessly as her forehead slammed against the concrete sidewalk. The sound was hideous, and I cried out.

My mother was able to roll onto her back. She stared at the

bright blue sky, unable to get up. I knelt beside her, horrified by the large knot that was forming in the middle of her forehead. I hoped it would be bandaged quickly and she wouldn't see it. But her fingers found the knot. She touched it gently, but seemed to be in shock and had no reaction. Dr. Mitchell would later say that the curb was about an inch too tall for her current ability to step up. I berated myself. I should have thought of that. I'm sure there was a different route we might have used, had I been less focused on projecting an image of the ideal daughter and more attentive to Mama's actual difficulties. *Not a single one of us is perfect,* I could imagine hearing my daddy say in my head. That was the only redemptive moment of the afternoon.

Oh, how I wished to have his counsel right now. Mama, injured and unable to get herself up, lay with her head and shoulders on the sidewalk. Her legs trailed into the parking lot. Just then, a young woman in her thirties pulled into the lot.

"Oh, my goodness!" she said. "Want me to send a doctor or nurse out?"

"Absolutely," I said. "You're an angel. *Malaika,* in Swahili, it would be." She looked at me strangely, but I was just grateful she had arrived.

Once in Dr. Mitchell's office, Mama was thoroughly examined, but we were no closer to finding out why Mama's walking had deteriorated so rapidly. I took Mama's arm gingerly as we left the doctor's office and walked to my van. I felt shaky on the drive back to the Hearth, but I managed to get her settled for a nap.

Later on that very afternoon, as I was in my kitchen downing Xanax with some sweet iced tea and feeling sorry for myself, I heard Giles's car pull up.

"How are your parents doing?" he asked as I appeared. Feeling paranoid, I wondered if news of Mama's fall had spread. "Especially your mother and those problems with her gait," he innocently added. "What have the medics found out?"

Panic nibbled at the edges of my seeming poise. "Mama and Daddy are doing very well," I answered, joining Giles beside the Neon's open trunk.

Hoping for a change of subject, I peered into the trunk and saw a cardboard box containing several plastic bags.

"Any news of Lok?" I asked.

"They have now notified Lok that she will have to submit to a DNA test," Giles said. "To show she is really our daughter, and not an impostor stealing someone else's identity."

The September sun was harsh, and reflected sharp shards of light against the bumpers of our vehicles. I used my hand to shade my eyes. Giles opened up one bag and pulled some blade-like leaves out by their pale white, stringy roots.

"I'm so sorry for the delay, Giles. I'm sure it's just a formality, though, and then Lok will be with you." Giles was quiet and I sensed he didn't want to talk more about it so I changed the subject. "I keep meaning to tell you how much my mother loves to hear about your progress in our yard, Giles."

"I like your mother very, very much," he said. "And I am going to plant more roses in her honor, somewhere in this yard.

Tell her that, and that I will escort her through this bright green grass to see them, very soon. What would she like?"

"Oh, any kind. She's not particular." But then, remembering, I said, "When I was growing up, we had these really pretty, deep red roses. They were very large, and had the sweetest scent. She loved to place them on our kitchen table. She would float them in a clear, cut-glass bowl. You know, it even seemed those roses made the food taste better."

"Flowers sweeten everything," Giles said, content that we agreed on this, at last.

"Well, I like all of these," I told him, surveying the load he'd brought in his trunk. "So if you want to plant them here, it's fine." By the time my voice broke, Giles had already turned toward me with a look of concern.

I could no longer pretend that everything was all right. "Giles, she fell at the doctor's office today and it was my fault. I was thinking about the wrong things and she tripped on the curb. She's okay, but she has a terrible knot on her forehead."

"I am sorry, Mrs. Wall," Giles said.

I looked into the distance. "She wanted to use your Kenyan cane, and why didn't I let her do that? It's touching how much she loves it. She told me that she was going to take it to a show-and-tell at Heathwood Hearth."

"I know," Giles said. "I was there."

"You were there, Giles?"

"I was making a delivery to Heathwood Hearth for the Garden Shoppe a couple of weeks ago, and I saw your mother. She asked if I would come back the next day to answer questions about the cane. Your mother appreciates fine things. She told the group that learning about other cultures is rather like traveling the world."

"Really, Giles? I'm glad to hear that. She has seemed so quiet lately. To tell the truth, I have been afraid that she's depressed. I wonder why she doesn't mention things like this to me. Perhaps I need to be a better listener, do you think?"

A few days later, I went to the Hearth to have lunch with my parents. Mama's head was still bandaged, and I told her that I had been wrong to advise her not to use Giles's cane. She should use it exactly as she saw fit, I said. Then I told her about the roses that Giles was planting for her in my yard—deep red roses, just like the ones back home.

10.

The Perfect Christmas Tree

My growing friendship with Giles was like a river that sometimes split into two separate streams, but always came back together again. We'd get busy with other things in our lives and follow our own paths for a while. With the arrival of winter there wasn't so much yard work to do, and Giles worked longer shifts at the grocery store, so days or a week might pass without our exchanging even a few words. But then when we saw each other again, we picked up right where we left off, as if we'd been saving up everything we had to say to each other, just waiting for an opportunity to spill.

Our conversations always started with family. I asked after Lok, he asked about my children and my parents. Then, inevitably, something would take us off on a flight of intellectual fancy, and we'd find ourselves immersed in a conversation about space and time and the theory of relativity. Whatever the subject matter, Giles seemed to know something about it. This was amazing and delightful to me. I had no other friend like him, no one else who was so willing and happy to ponder such things along with me. Fate had sent a professor to my door, and my conversations with him were like a dream class—we didn't talk about anything that didn't interest us, and there was absolutely no homework.

I'd been a good student in school, but no one had ever accused me of being an intellectual. In truth, no one would have wanted me to be—when I was young, girls weren't pushed to excel academically. A girl who got a 4.0 average might as well have hung a sign on her chest that said: "Doomed Never to Marry." There were two career choices that were considered acceptable for girls: teacher or nurse. One day in high school, the boys and girls were divided into groups to talk about our future aspirations. Our guidance counselor, a woman with hair teased so high that it practically scraped the ceiling, asked all of us girls to write on a form what we wanted to be when we grew up. I dutifully wrote "Teacher." My friend wrote "Doctor." When the guidance counselor walked around collecting the forms she made my friend erase "Doctor" and change it to "Nurse."

I considered myself a life-long learner with a curious mind, but I'd been perfectly satisfied to stop my formal education after college. Over the years, as the kids were growing up, I occasionally wondered what might have happened if I had chosen another path—maybe a master's in English or even a Ph.D., leading to a job as a professor. But those were idle musings—I knew myself well enough to know that graduate school would never have been for me. I was a happy dilettante, and I loved following my own nose, picking up books on topics as they interested me. As soon as someone else told me what I had to study, it sucked the joy right out of it for me. So my conversations with Dr. Giles Owita became my ideal postgraduate education. I even took notes.

I could see that Giles also enjoyed our conversations. As he answered my questions, the cadence in his voice would change. He couldn't hide the joy he found in teaching, and at times like that I had to stop myself from saying out loud how shortsighted those universities had been in not hiring him. His talent for explaining concepts that could otherwise be dreary or far too difficult always amazed me, so I made it a habit to ask him about anything that flew way over my head. One time, I'd been reading a biography of Einstein, and had been mulling one of his trickier thought experiments.

"Giles, I'm confused. I just finished reading about the passenger riding on the train that's struck by lightning. I still don't understand why the person on the train and the person on the platform see two different things, and what exactly that proves."

Just as I knew he would, Giles warmed to the subject with relish and announced that he was going to look for one of his college texts that would help me better understand the concept. He said he would loan it to me, and I felt honored, as if I had been promoted from beginner to intermediate.

I thought about this as I drove into town a few weeks before Christmas. Giles had given me so much since our friendship had begun a year and a half before. I wondered what I could ever give him in return. As happy as he always was to see me, I couldn't believe that he got nearly as much as I did from our conversations. Each time I walked away from Giles, I felt either enlightened by his brilliance or unburdened of some of my worries and sadness. I wished I could do the same for him.

It was after dark and flakes of snow swirled as I pulled into a downtown parking lot beside the Farmer's Market. Dick was supposed to meet me there after work to look at Christmas trees. Stars twinkled from the velvet depths of night. Strands of colored Christmas lights zigzagged up and down the length of Market Street. Pulled into the festive atmosphere, I paused at cheery store windows decorated with familiar scenes of reindeer in the snow or children peering down the stairs to see what Santa brought.

I heard a woman's voice calling my name. It was Elaine, the biology teacher at school. She held a clutch of pine boughs in her hand. We exchanged greetings, and I told her that I was on a hunt for a tree.

"You should buy one from Giles," she said. "He's over there, across the street. Apparently, his son is on a travel soccer team, and they're doing it as a fund-raiser."

I held a hand up. "Stop! We've been there!" I laughingly

explained all the brownies, candy bars, and boxes of flavored popcorn I'd sold from metal folding tables in various commercial parking lots over the years. Not to mention the yard sales. All in the service of one of the kids' sports teams.

"Say hi to Giles for me," Elaine said as she ran off with her boughs. She was yet another of Giles's many fans, ever since I'd passed his name along to her after she'd told me that her yard was suffering from the drought. I wondered anew how Giles managed to do everything he did—hold down multiple jobs, work for more and more private clients, and sell Christmas trees for his son's soccer team. I spotted the handmade sign across the street where fir trees held their arms out, catching snowflakes.

ROANOKE COMETS

STATE SOCCER CHAMPIONS . . . DIVISION 3-A

. . . HELP US GO TO NATIONALS!

I scanned the soccer booth for any sign of Giles. Then a six-foot pine with perfect symmetry attracted my eye.

There was one person manning the booth, his back to me. From the shape of him, I suspected he was one of the soccer players—he was tall enough to seem fully grown, but he had the sinewy build of a teenager. "Excuse me. Could I see this one?"

The tree was loosely tied with string and leaned back toward a support post. Above where it rested, a canvas awning had filled up with snow. I pulled my winter gloves off, fingering the fragrant needles as more falling snow sifted through the leafless branches of the maple trees that lined the street.

The boy who turned around looked familiar, and I realized immediately that he must be Giles's son. He was indeed in his teens and towered over me. His smile was just as electric as his father's. "Sure," he said to me. "I like that one, myself. Let me stand it up for you. The branches fall just right. It's almost like a Christmas card."

"Are you Dr. Giles Owita's son?" I impulsively asked the boy.

He paused, seeming uncomfortable, the way any teenage boy would be when put on the spot.

"Your father is a friend of ours. And he does some landscape work for us as well."

"Oh, right. He's pretty good at that. I'm Naam."

"I'm Carol Wall," I said. "My husband and I just love your dad's work."

We shook hands.

"Is your brother here as well, and your mom?"

"Yes, ma'am. They're selling wreaths. Across the street, and farther down. You see?"

The falling snow created a temporary scrim, yet soon it slowed to yield a vision of Bienta huddled at a table strewn with greenery and wreaths and velvet bows for sale.

Naam took some pruning shears and snipped the string from the tree. I resisted the temptation to embarrass him further by telling him that I'd been hearing all about him and his siblings for some time. Instead, I focused on the way the pine tree branches quivered as they settled into shape.

"Oh, it's beautiful," I said. "I'd like to buy it."

He took my folded bills. Then I saw Giles advancing toward us from about a block away. His footsteps were energetic as he hurried down the sidewalk from the coffee shop. "Here's Dad," Naam said.

"Hot chocolate!" Giles announced, balancing several cups in a paper carrier. He handed one to his son, then smiled at me.

"Would you like a hot chocolate, Mrs. Wall?"

"Oh. No thanks. Dick is taking me out for a sandwich soon, and I don't want to spoil my appetite. Are you taking one over to Bienta? Do you mind if I walk over with you? I'd love to say hello."

Giles nodded and said of course, but I noticed he stiffened a bit and grew guarded. I'd noticed lately that he often did that when the subject of Bienta arose. I knew that the loss of a child could hit spouses in different ways, sometimes causing a rift. I wondered if their separation from Lok had done the same to them. Giles always went out of his way to praise Bienta and how accomplished she was, but it seemed to me that there was a wistfulness to the way he spoke about Bienta, a sadness mixed with his admiration. He had told me how she'd managed a farm in Kenya, and how in her work as a nurse she had delivered two babies with nothing but a lantern to find the mothers' huts and a razor blade to cut the umbilical cords. Bienta was an amazing woman, and Giles was a remarkable man. In so many ways they seemed perfectly suited to each other. But life had brought them so many disappointments.

When we reached Bienta, she smiled politely. "How is your mother?"

"My mother is somewhat better, thank you. Her spirits are good."

Giles extended a cup of hot chocolate toward Bienta after having carefully wrapped a napkin around it to absorb the heat. I watched as she shook her head, her body turned away. He was clearly eager to please her, and I felt uneasy, as if I had stumbled onto a private conversation that wasn't going well.

I introduced myself to Wath, their younger son. He was shorter than Naam and had a more compact build. His eyelashes were long and his expression held a merry aspect that reminded me of Giles. Yet he seemed more instantly at ease, more outgoing and chatty than either his brother or his father. He exuded the confidence of a well-loved youngest child.

I bought a wreath from Bienta, as well as a red ribbon from Wath. Across the street, Naam had wrapped my lovely pine tree with twine and called to his dad for help in carrying it to my van.

"I may be calling or writing you soon. About my parents," I said to Bienta in parting, "if you don't mind me taking advantage of some of your nursing expertise."

"I would love to be of help," she said, and I felt she meant it.

A few minutes later, as Giles fit the tree into the van, I asked him, "How have you been?" He produced string to tie the hatch down.

"I'm very well," he said.

He took off his heavy gloves in order to tie the string. As I watched him work, I glimpsed a scar on the side of his wrist, which in all our time together I had never noticed. The scar was three or four inches long and slightly jagged. "My God, what happened to your wrist, Giles?"

He looked at the scar and his eyes grew narrow, as if he'd forgotten and needed to refresh his memory. Then he blinked, his lids two tranquil-looking crescent shapes. "I had a melanoma. This was several years ago, in Blacksburg. A course of treatment was prescribed."

"Surgery?"

"Yes. Removal of the mole and some surrounding tissue."

Giles had cancer? I struggled to fit this new information into the image I had formed of Giles as the picture of health. I took a moment to reimagine him leaping into my birch tree, but this time he missed his mark and fell to the ground. It gave me a chill, and I shrank farther into my wool overcoat.

"I just can't believe that you had melanoma, Giles." The words came quickly, and as quickly, I regretted that I'd spoken them. They sounded accusatory, somehow. Just exactly like what a casual acquaintance, Ella, had said to me at church at the time of my cancer diagnosis. She had spoken in a tone of voice more suited to addressing someone who'd been caught stealing money from the collection plate. "You, Carol? Oh no! You've always seemed so healthy. I never would have thought it. Your voice is strong and it carries so well from the loft. Are you a vegetarian? You seem to exercise a lot. Were you breast-fed as a baby?"

"No and no," I'd said, stifling a laugh, which may have been what saved me from killing her.

Now I realized that my own tone of voice betrayed a note of shock that really had as much (or more) to do with fears for myself as it did with Giles. It was scary when a healthy, able man like Giles had cancer. Just like Ella had done with me, I struggled to make sense of it, to come up with something that Giles might have done—or not done—to cause it. I of all people should have known better, and yet here I was doing the same ignorant thing that I'd railed against since my own diagnosis. Cancer was a disease, not a judgment, and we were all at risk— in spite of our healthy habits.

Finally, I ventured another question. "Did you have to have chemo?"

"A course of chemotherapy was recommended. That's true enough. I did not welcome it. In fact, I stopped before its course had run. After the first chemotherapy treatment, I could see it interfered with working, and I had a family to feed. So I told them I would not be back. This did not stop the scheduler from calling me, every time, and when I answered, she would give me my appointment time and place. And with each and every call, my answer was the same. 'Thank you very much. I will not be there!'"

He chuckled at the memory, shaking his head with an air of

wry amusement. Apparently, he had not elaborated on his answer to that chemo scheduler. He had just offered his polite decline in his usual lilting tone, as if he were simply turning down a second cup of coffee.

The nurse probably thought she was dealing with a prankster or a man with a mental problem. I couldn't help myself. I laughed out loud along with Giles. "I will not be there!" I said, repeating his words while shaking my own head in amazement. He looked at his cancer treatment as if he'd had a choice about it, as if it were a restaurant menu and no one could force him to eat what he didn't want. Lord knew that had never occurred to me. My Handsome Oncologist had said that cancer patients are generally exceedingly compliant. They might not like a particular treatment; nonetheless, desperate to be well, they did as told. Apparently, Giles was one of the exceptions.

I gave Giles some extra dollar bills for the boys to use on their trip. Still thinking of his decision about the chemo, I felt giddy as I imagined alarm bells sounding at his doctor's office, and an APB extending all through Blacksburg and areas surrounding. "Be on the lookout for an educated cancer patient who chose not to pick his poison!"

I let my head fall back, startled by the very notion of laughter flying from my deepest heart. Joy was an emotion I had never associated with cancer. Yet Giles seemed to find a place for joy in all of life's experiences. He reminded me of a gambler at the table with his last chip. He would enjoy the game until the final deal.

This was a whole new idea for me. The freedom held in just one second of realizing that everybody in this world is going to live until they die brought tears to my eyes. My cancer didn't put me in a special category, I told myself. Like everyone, I would live until I died (perhaps because of cancer, or perhaps it would be from something else, like a Coca-Cola truck barreling through an intersection).

I took a tissue from my purse to wipe my eyes, giggling to recall how Dick resisted vitamins his doctor ordered for him, explaining that he would have to "read up more." He scanned all the labels on his food and wrote down his weight from week to week on special index cards. He lived in the illusion of control. It was very understandable but also quite annoying. And how I'd missed that illusion for myself. It seemed a thousand years had passed since I'd last felt bulletproof.

But what I'd missed the most was simply being Carol, without the postscript "cancer survivor" added to my name.

Giles was silent. We folded our cancer diagnoses into our list of things in common. The difference was, Giles acted like it was the least among his problems.

"With practice, possibly, I'll learn to be like you," I told him.

"No, not like me," he protested, and an unexpected cloud crossed his face.

"You're quite amazing. Did you know that, Giles? Everybody says so."

Suddenly, he seemed aware of being cold. He brushed off the

snow accumulating on his cap and along the shoulders of his jacket. He stamped his boots to free them of the packed-on ice.

I gave a grateful wave to Giles and walked toward the bookstore where I was meeting Dick. Giles went in the opposite direction, back toward the Christmas tree lot.

I felt a peace I hadn't experienced in ages. I wasn't alone. We're often told that, but in this moment I was able to believe it. I turned around to catch another glimpse of Giles, and saw my footprints filling up with snow. When I turned back, Dick had crossed the street and was walking toward me.

"What's happened?" he said.

"What do you mean?"

"You look different. Good. Did you get your hair cut?"

"No. It's just . . ." I heard carolers in the distance. Their voices mingled beautifully, I tried to think of a way to explain this feeling to Dick, but I couldn't. So I simply said, "I found the perfect Christmas tree."

II.

Frail Magnolia

I t was the wee hours of Sunday morning, the week before
Christmas. I stood under a giant clock whose sweeping second hand was like a cricket leaping with mechanical precision
over every centimeter of the unforgiving hours. Dick was with
me, and an ER doctor faced us within the bowels of Valley
Hospital.

My mother battled for her life. She had been brought in by
ambulance at about midnight after falling in her apartment. It
was a stroke. Dr. Bell, the neurologist on call, let us see the
scan. An ugly continent of blood spread through her brain tissue, with the evidence of damage still evolving.

An hour ago, IVs installed, she had roused herself to say good
night to me. I asked how she was feeling, and she answered,

without conviction, "Okay, I guess." But as the sun came up, I noticed her face drooped more, and she could no longer speak. Her right side was paralyzed.

Just the week before in their apartment at the Hearth, I had shared in the fun of helping Mama wrap a stack of Christmas presents for her grandchildren. Daddy wandered a bit, but he seemed to have a sense of purpose, and to feel some engagement with the familiar holiday activities.

Mama had always loved Christmas. We worked together by her bed, which we'd transformed into a wrapping table. Her fingernails were almond-shaped, and perfect, painted with pale peach polish she'd applied herself. Here in the hospital, in the hours after her stroke, the polish had been unceremoniously removed because they needed to see her nail beds.

Dr. Bell spoke to me of stabilizing Mama. She'd have to do a "swallow test" to see if she could handle solid food. Then she would start physical therapy as soon as possible. Dr. Bell maintained eye contact with me, but the note of resignation in his voice told me a lot.

I had tried to seem alert as Dr. Bell continued talking, but my mind wandered to the phone call I'd received from the nurse at the Hearth shortly after midnight. Daddy had found Mama on the floor. Her speech was garbled. In a single effort that made sense, he found the nurse. "My wife needs help. I tried to pick her up, but she can't talk and things aren't working very well." His puzzled, blinking eyes were all too easy for me to imagine. Almost everything else behind them had been emptied out, but in Mama's hour of need he'd come to her rescue, just as he always had.

Now I followed Mama's gurney to an upstairs floor, where she'd been assigned another room. Christmas cutouts decorated the walls. We passed sad-looking poinsettias sitting at a bank of windows in the hallway.

I waited outside while they settled my mother in her new room. My purse hung heavy on one shoulder and my mother's purse dangled from the other. I thought of how she'd tripped in Dr. Mitchell's parking lot when I was supposed to be watching her. I wondered if she'd ever carry this purse again, and if our chatter would ever again fill a room or set the phone lines buzzing.

Soon, the nurse came out. "All right," she said. "You can go in now."

I went inside and stood beside the bed. Mama looked like she was only sleeping. Feeling oddly disconnected from the scene, I wondered if I was morphing into someone terrible, a stranger to myself—a power of attorney, next of kin, whose primary emotion was shameful relief to be the one who was upright, well, and whole.

Then inspiration struck. I took a piece of paper out of a zipper compartment of my purse and softly said, "Mama, here are Giles's recent plans. He calls it *Mrs. Wall's Wildflower Garden*. Here is his description: 'Location: backyard . . . adjacent to birdbath. Border to be built with stones (kite) from the river (arora)— *Rudbeckia hirta* (black-eyed Susan), *Trillium undulatum* (painted trillium), *Silene virginica* (fire pink), *Cypripedium acaule* (lady's slipper).'"

Sensing that she heard me, I paused. I felt my voice about to break, and yet I hurried forward. "Mama, this is going to happen in the spring. It will be a smaller version of Sarah Driscoll's meditation garden. Giles will do the hard work. You and I will sip our sweet iced tea and supervise. Rhudy will curl up under your chair, so happy to see you. Now, don't forget!"

Her eyeballs raced beneath lids that now seemed parchment-thin. The fingers of her good hand flickered briefly, where they rested against the starched white sheets. It was tempting to imagine she might weave my words into a pleasant dream of flowers in an earthly garden somewhere that was yet to be.

Giles stopped by our house one evening while Mama was in the hospital to deliver a steaming pot of beef stew and a dish of rice from Bienta. Giles said that the stew was called *Pilau* in Swahili. Bienta took great pride in the secret spices she added to her version of the dish, and she didn't give her recipe out to many people, he explained. "But, with you, she is making this exception. You have had so much stress with your mother. And you were kind enough to help the soccer team raise funds. Please keep the contents of this envelope strictly to yourself. Bienta has taped this to the pan for you."

"No problem," I said. "I'm an excellent keeper of secrets."

Dick and Giles started into the kitchen to warm the stew. I

followed them and gently pulled Bienta's secret envelope from under the tape on the lid of the heavy metal pan.

"I will call Bienta with my thanks," I said to Giles.

"That is not necessary," he quickly insisted, once again taking on that tone of nervousness I'd come to associate with him and Bienta. "I will tell her how pleased you are."

Once Giles left, I read Bienta's letter.

Dear Mrs. Wall,

I have been pondering a very important question that affects my family. For some time, I have felt troubled and have, from our first introduction, wanted to speak with you in confidence. Believing, as I do, that my husband's trust in you is well founded, I would like to request about an hour of your time for a meeting at my house. I will arrange a time when the boys and Giles will be away, as I want them to know nothing of this matter until a decision is made. Would Tuesday afternoon of next week be convenient for you? If you could stop by after school, I would appreciate it so much. Below are directions to our house. My family's secret spices for the stew are included on the back of this card.

Gratefully,

Bienta Owita

I turned on the backyard spotlights and then stood at the kitchen window, rereading the note. If only she had given more clues. Clearly, the family's spices for the stew weren't the only secret being kept here.

. . .

I walked down the Owitas' sidewalk on the scheduled afternoon, my arms encircling Bienta's stew pot. The winter air was
dry, I was four minutes early, and my nerves were on edge. The
note on the stew pot read something like a summons.

My winter boots made prints across the frosty grass of
the Owitas' landscaped yard. A picture window at the front of
the house offered a hazy glimpse of Christmas cactus and poinsettias.

The pot was heavy and I shifted it onto my hip and rang the
bell. After a time, Bienta answered.

"Hello," she greeted me, polite and guarded as always. Her
eyes went to the empty stew pot.

"It was absolutely wonderful," I said. "And your secret spices
are safe with me."

Her face grew just a little milder, and I felt myself relax a
notch as well.

"Please do come in," she said.

Once inside I said, "Bienta, you have kept me in suspense too
long. Is everything okay?"

"Okay? Of course! What would be wrong?"

"Well," I said, fishing for a plausible answer, "I guess I was
thinking of Lok."

"Lok is fine. There is nothing new to report."

"Last summer, I snipped three roses from Sarah's meditation

garden and pressed them. I will give you one so you can send it to Lok. Giles says it's her favorite flower."

"That would be very nice," Bienta said. She looked toward the bookcase in their living room, full of photographs of happy times.

Bienta's hair was wrapped in silky fabric patterned in brown and black and white. She was dressed elegantly in a long-sleeved blouse and flowing, floor-length skirt. By contrast, my boots and jeans and belted leather jacket looked distinctly L.L.Bean. I envied her grace and femininity. It seemed to come naturally to her, whereas I always felt that I had to work a little too hard at it. "You look so beautiful," I said.

"I am going to a wedding shower later in the afternoon," she said. "Please, tell me how your mother is."

"She's about the same. The doctor says it will take time."

I scanned the bookshelves and assorted photos. One captured Lok, age five or six, posing on the shores of Lake Victoria. A blue sky stretches endlessly above the dull green surface of the placid water. Another picture showed Giles in a white lab coat, out in a field in Kenya, it appeared. He is surrounded by a dozen young men holding up large cabbages.

Bienta invited me to sit. I chose the sofa, but she settled for an uncomfortable wooden chair that faced me.

"There is something I would like to ask you," she said. She pulled an index card from the pocket of her skirt and consulted it briefly. There was writing on both sides. "There are so many things I need to talk about. The school where you teach, Saint Benedict's. Your children went there. Yes?"

"Oh. Yes. They did. All three of them are graduates."

"So, you would recommend it highly, I would guess? We are thinking about it for our boys."

Relief rendered me limp. School was an easy subject compared to whatever mysterious question I was dreading. "I would recommend it highly. Yes," I confirmed. "And if your boys attend, maybe I'll be lucky enough to be their English teacher someday!"

"Oh, indeed. That would be nice." Once again she removed the card from her pocket and took her time studying it. Her expression turned cloudy. "Your mother," she said. "Tell me more. You mentioned that you might want my advice. I have worked with many stroke patients."

"My mother . . ." I started to say, but stopped and tried again. "She looks so terrible," I blurted out. "And I know in my heart that she'll never be the same. Recently, she's started closing her eyes when I come into the room. It's almost as if she's angry with me and can't bear to look at me."

"This is very, very normal. In my nursing I have seen such situations many times. Your mother has both receptive and expressive aphasia. That is very limiting. She strikes out at you because she knows you will understand and love her, no matter what. I know it sounds counterintuitive, but try to think of this as a compliment, in the same way that a child would run to place her head on her mother's lap when she is upset. She has always been able to count on you. Yes?"

"Yes."

I felt relief at finally admitting my selfish fears about Mama. Then immediately I felt envy once again. Bienta sat in front of me, serene and calm, as if she could face anything and emerge with her dignity intact. It's how I would like to be.

Bienta stood to point out photos of the children growing up. Then she came to her wedding picture.

"Dick and I married young, as well," I said. "And have been very happy, too, except for the usual spats and misunderstandings."

She offered no response.

I felt myself growing frustrated, as if I'd been tested without knowing it and had failed miserably. "I've been talking too much. I think there must be something else you wanted to ask me about." I stopped talking and this time I pledged to be the one to wait quietly until Bienta filled the silence.

"I've told no one," she began, and then hesitated. She paused and placed a hand on the table for balance. Her expression was troubled. Was she afraid of something or someone? She suddenly looked up toward the front of the house. "Wait. Did you hear a car?"

We both startled when Giles burst through the door. He wore a pair of neat-pressed khakis and a heavy jacket only partly zipped. The navy collar of his Foodland shirt was sticking out.

His schedule had been "rearranged," he explained. He had noticed my car parked outside and was delighted to see me.

"The boys are still at practice," he said to Bienta. "It will be ninety minutes more."

"Oh. All right. Of course. I'll pick them up," she said. Her tone was cool and closed again. It seemed as if every time I got close to penetrating Bienta's shell, something came along and she shut herself up tight again. "In any case, I have some errands now."

It struck me that she suddenly seemed almost frantic to get away. In her rush, she dropped her car keys. As she scooped them from the floor, I noticed how her fingers trembled.

"We were speaking of my mother," I broke in to say. "Bienta has been so helpful, giving me welcome perspective based on her experience."

"Oh, yes," Giles readily responded, looking toward Bienta, his eyes sparkling with genuine regard and admiration. "Bienta always has the answer."

"I should go," I announced.

"Perhaps you'd like to show Mrs. Wall your backyard projects when she leaves," Bienta suggested.

"I'm really short on time," I said. My nervous fingers went to my knotted belt to pull it tighter. "In the next few days, I'll pick up some brochures for you, Bienta. About Saint B's."

Bienta thanked me and left, then Giles escorted me through the kitchen and out the back door to a barren stretch of grass, which, unaccountably, he seemed quite happy with. Bright blue tarps covered much of the yard, and what was exposed looked blank and lifeless to my eyes. As I strolled, pretending to admire the view, I wondered what surprised me more—the untended state of Giles's backyard, or the obvious tensions in the Owitas' marriage.

Giles led me toward a small magnolia on the far side of his slightly tilting garden shed. "This is from a shoot of the magnolia tree in Mrs. Driscoll's yard." Giles trapped a bloom between two fingers and held it out for me to see.

"Yes. I see. It's pretty, and I know it will be happy here," I said.

"In Blacksburg, which is in the mountains, it's too cold for a magnolia. But here, in our fertile valley, with the air a little warmer and more humid, such a tree may well exceed its normal upper limits."

"Like my river birch?" I said.

"Exactly right," he answered me, his optimistic face turned toward the clouds, as if he had nothing to fear.

He walked me halfway to the van, but paused to press his fingers on the frozen soil, evaluating something unidentified. As I drove away, I stole a glimpse of him striding toward his garden gate with a light step.

It struck me as deeply strange that he should feel so proud of his lackluster backyard with its bright blue tarps, frail magnolia tree, and a garden shed that looked like it had seen better days. Given Giles's talent, how could this have happened? Perhaps the answer lay in the collective subconscious of a family displaced.

The fertile front yard reflected the family's happy public face and the barren area out back expressed the unhappiness they hid from view.

I was surely overanalyzing. I needed Dick to tell me that I was being ridiculous. Perhaps the Owitas just preferred to spend their money and their efforts in front, where passersby could enjoy the view. Somehow, I knew that the truth wasn't so simple. I recalled the index card Bienta had guarded in her skirt pocket. I saw her trembling fingers reaching for the car keys and her troubled expression. There was anguish in that house, and I didn't know why.

12.

Lemon

My mother's recovery from her stroke was slow, but by the first warm days of spring, I started to feel optimistic again. At least I didn't worry every time I walked away from Mama that I might never see her again. So Dick and I decided to treat ourselves to a three-day getaway to our favorite mountain inn in North Carolina.

The weekend went well, and we both felt refreshed on the drive home. Dick complimented me on my low-cut cotton sweater and admired my newly purchased blue jean skirt. We laughed to think how shocked our kids would be if they suspected we were still in love in the standard, hearts-and-flowers way, despite our creaking joints and gray hair.

Occasionally, I looked over at Dick and admired his handsome profile and his strong, freckled forearms. We'd now been together significantly more than half our lives, but I hadn't ever tired of him. That was one positive by-product of my jealous nature, I supposed. I never took him for granted. I brushed my fingers through his combed-back, silvery hair. Whenever he complained of growing bald, I always assured him that I thought it made him look distinguished. After all these years, the secret to our success was really pretty simple. He was still my guy.

When I was twenty, beginning my sophomore year in college, my parents gave their consent for me to marry Dick, who was a year behind me in school. Dick's parents were thrilled, and I suppose the unspoken understanding was that at least we were doing things in the right order—marriage first, pregnancy later. In a small town like Radford, people pulled out their calendars when a young bride started showing, doing their quick, nosy math to figure out if the bride and groom had really waited until their wedding night.

In high school, Dick had been known as a liberal trouble-maker whose family came from somewhere up North. He wore wire-rimmed glasses when they were practically synonymous with being a hippie, and he let his hair grow long and scruffy, so it touched his ears. Worse, he made no secret of his dislike for LBJ, and he clearly hadn't been born saying "yes, ma'am" and "no, sir" the way the rest of us good Southern children had been. He'd even been one of two white students to join with all the black students in our high school to protest the playing of "Dixie" by the marching band at the start of each pep rally.

They all walked out of the school gymnasium en masse, and that damn song was never played at a pep rally again.

None of the above presented a problem for my parents. In fact, they admired Dick for his beliefs. But it definitely gave Mama a gulp of concern that Dick was—gasp—a Catholic. It was downright comical to imagine it now, but this was at a time when being Catholic was seen as something exotic, even heretical, in my tiny, blinkered town. Folks had vague associations with mystical-sounding incantations and praying to statues. Still, to her credit, Mama got past her hesitation, and it was agreed that Dick and I would be married by a priest in my parents' Methodist church. It was an icy January day, but the church was packed. It seemed that a lot of local Protestants were willing to loosen their Bible Belts long enough to see what kind of razzle-dazzle might be brought to bear by a Catholic priest.

Dick and I drove a little while in silence. The passing scenery flew by, a tapestry of mingled, woodsy greens. Inside my head, a butterfly of worry landed. I couldn't help fearing that I would arrive home to news that Mama or Daddy had taken a downturn.

"Remember when the kids were small?" I said to Dick. "I always had this urge to check in with the babysitter, and you would try to talk me out of it."

"Yep. Exactly right. But I was never successful, so you called and then felt better for about twelve hours. Then the cycle would begin again."

Dick fiddled with the radio dial and finally found a station he approved of. It was an oldies station, and "Baby Love" was playing. I sang along, providing backup, and he graciously refrained from asking me to stop. Settling back, he readjusted his sunglasses, and I thought of the days when we were our younger and more slender selves, with thicker hair and whiter teeth and much more energy. Growing older was no picnic, but our nearly thirty-five years of marriage was something to be proud of. I felt a surge of satisfaction knowing that our parents' wisdom in giving us their blessing had been confirmed. Our parents weren't crazy, and our detractors had it wrong. Dick and I had stood the test of time.

As we turned onto Mount Vernon Road, the neighborhood looked different. It seemed the grass had grown a little thicker, even in these past few days. Surprisingly, pink flowers set on leafless stalks had bloomed beside the driveway. I gave a little gasp as we pulled in. How lovely the flowers were, what an unexpected pleasure.

Dick and I each grabbed handfuls of bags to bring into the house, and I managed to be first to our mailbox, where I saw a slim white envelope waiting for me. The return address was the imaging center where I went for my regular mammograms. I'd gone in a few weeks prior to our trip and had hoped to get the results before we left. But no such luck.

I hadn't said a word about it to Dick, but despite the pleasure I took in our time away, the arrival of this envelope had occupied a hidden corner of my mind throughout our trip. Whether we were shopping or relaxing, sleeping late or being pampered in the spa, I felt its presence in its absence. Now it was here.

I would recognize the imaging center's bright blue logo anywhere, and I knew that Dick would as well. I wondered if he remembered that it was that time of year again. In my head, I did the math: thirteen days between the mammogram and when we left on vacation. Surely they would have phoned me by now if there were a problem. Once, after the lumpectomy, I did have to go back for extra pictures, but everything turned out okay, I reminded myself.

I didn't want Dick to know the news contained in the envelope before I did. Why worry Dick, I thought to myself, when only minutes later, I could scan the contents and then announce, with dignity, that we were off the hook again?

But just as my fingers grasped the envelope with the bright blue return address, Dick's hand went over mine and we struggled for control over that slim piece of paper.

He, too, recognized the blue return address. Lewis-Gale Medical Center, Department of Radiology. Later, he confessed that he had read my calendar and knew exactly when I had my mammogram. He'd held his vigil on vacation, too. So, even in our closest times, it was something that came between us despite the fact that neither of us acknowledged it to the other. The beautiful green eyes that had looked at me with love only a short time earlier now held an empty look, as if he were bracing himself.

I somehow managed to snatch the envelope out of his hand. Without the envelope to hold on to, Dick looked even more forlorn, lacking even an illusion of control over the situation. He turned the key to our front-door lock. I twisted the knob. As I held the envelope away from him, I thought of all our bags of purchases from our weekend shopping trip. My favorite was a pair of black velvet shoes that reminded me of Audrey Hepburn. Maybe I'd surprise everyone and die in style.

In the foyer now, I turned toward Dick abruptly.

"Here," I said. "Take it. You're the head of this household. Read it to me."

Reluctantly, he accepted it. As I stepped back, my purse knocked something off the narrow table in the hall. It was a picture of Dick's parents in their younger days. Full of remorse, I picked it up. The glass was broken, but the photo was intact and could be reframed. I looked up and saw Dick and me reflected in the gilded oval mirror that had come from my grandmother's house. I noticed the veins that stood out on Dick's neck like cords, the jutting motion of his handsome jaw, the blood that rushed to transform his face into a mask of rage that covered up an even deeper feeling: fear. Fear of losing.

"Here, Carol. You read it. I'm sorry," Dick said. "The news will be good. Let's get to that part, okay?"

"You know how I hate that happy talk—right?" Poor Dick. He couldn't win for losing. My fingers ripped the paper in a single motion, and I scanned the contents. *Dear Carol Wall: Your recent mammogram* . . . it began, and then, within the space of several seconds, I felt like the heroine in one of those old movies, standing on the window ledge of a twenty-story building as the crowd below gathers to watch the spectacle.

I pulled out a dining room chair and sat down.

"It isn't good," I said.

"What do you mean?"

"It's the other breast this time. The 'healthy' one. They want me to come back for another mammogram."

"Oh, God."

"I told you," I said, clutching my stomach. As my composure crumbled, Dick's eyes grew hard. I stifled several silent sobs. Pressure built against my diaphragm.

"Now, listen," he began to lecture, pacing to and fro as if delivering his closing arguments to a moot court jury. "You can't get all worked up about each wrinkle in the process. You've had cancer . . ."

I picked at my fingernails, doing my very best to come across as a grown-up who had received some mildly disappointing news. I blinked rapidly to hold back tears. "Really, Dick? What part of my breast cancer felt like merely a wrinkle to you? Having a part of my body removed? Lying on a table as everyone else scampered out before my dose of radiation was turned on?"

Dick put his hands on my shoulders. He tried to project a calm voice. "What I meant was, Carol, first we have to get a handle on what we're dealing with. We can't react to every little thing that happens. You'll just go back and let them take some further pictures. They're being careful. Don't we want them to be?"

"We?" I screamed, losing composure. "It's somewhere you can't go. What do you do when I have surgery? You get a cup of coffee, read the paper in the waiting room. When they did the biopsy, you even gave them your cell number and had them call you at the office. You racked up some billable hours while I was being knifed. Can't you get this through your head? The love between us, our kids and our home, have been the center of our lives since we were barely old enough to vote. *This* threatens it. The worst part is, we can't control the outcome. Your being so healthy is going to come between us. I just know it will. I already feel left out, unworthy and resentful. Wait and see."

Dick looked stunned. He ran his fingers through his hair. He looked at the lovely Oriental rug that anchored the dining room table and chairs. We bought it in Richmond some years back, on a getaway trip when the kids were small. The rug's colors had mellowed over time, reminding me of the life Dick and I had lived together for over thirty years. I thought of our three children, and the games they'd played on this rug, the milk and cookie crumbs they'd spilled on it. We'd all left our mark.

"We've always had a lot to lose," I said, feeling remorseful for my outburst.

"I know," he said.

"I can't be calm about something like this, Dick. I'm not like you that way."

Dick got a faraway look on his face as I began thinking how I hated that place, the radiology department. It was like being in the grave . . . no windows . . . cold. It had even occurred to me at a particularly morbid moment that they might as well have situated the morgue nearby, conveniently close after they'd finished scaring you to death. Everyone was so nice there, so supportive. But the thought that they knew something about me that I didn't know yet made me crazy.

My thoughts of illness and death inevitably brought me back to my childhood. All roads led me there. I remembered the time Daddy, Judy, and I were diagnosed with the polio virus. I was probably five years old at the time. Daddy was in the hospital for a short time. Meanwhile, the rest of us were quarantined in the house. The crisis soon passed, but it took its toll on Mama. One day after Daddy returned to work, she had what must have been a panic attack. She lay on the sofa and told me to call Daddy at work. This had never, ever happened, and instinctively I knew that it was my job to remain calm, and to try to keep Mama calm until Daddy arrived. So while Mama lay on the sofa, holding one hand over her heart, I sat on the floor beside her and pretended to read the comics. And that's when things got really strange. When Daddy got home, he and Mama decided that the way to draw the least amount of attention from the neighbors was to avoid calling an ambulance. So instead, they called Daddy's friend who owned a funeral home and asked him to send a hearse for Mama. And while Judy and I stood on the front porch, two junior honor guards, they rolled Mama by us on a gurney and down the steps to slide her into the hearse. To this day I wonder what on earth to make of that incident. Was Mama more afraid of illness than death? For my own part, I knew that I was deathly afraid of both.

"I need to get some air," Dick said. "As soon as you get your appointment, please let me know." Before I could respond, he snatched up his keys again. "There are a couple of things I need to check at the office."

I watched him screech away in his car, and instead of feeling abandoned, I was relieved to see him go. Dick and I needed to be away from each other for a few hours. Right now we only reminded each other of how much we had to lose, and how terrified we were. Then, as if it had been planned, I spotted Giles driving his Neon down our street.

Dick's car was gone, and Giles probably thought we weren't yet home from our trip. Peering out, I watched as he went straight to work along the flower bed he had built in front, between the boxwoods, where great heaps of orange and purple impatiens had erupted into pleasing mounds of color. There were also two small rosebushes, one for Lok and one for Mama.

From the kitchen window moments later, I watched as he inspected the wildflower garden we had just created by the birdbath. The stones were smooth, well worn by water flowing over time, and they encircled flowers that seemed content to be loosely organized, their blossoms tipping here and there, and even intertwining. There were lady's slippers, black-eyed Susans, painted trilliums, and so on. He did everything the way he had promised.

A shadow from the dogwood made a pattern on the grass as Giles moved on to check the creek bank. He paused, now and then, leaning down to pluck a leaf or use his hands to scatter soil. Why couldn't I be serene, like him?

Our house seemed too quiet. Rhudy had been staying in doggie care all week, so I didn't have him to distract me. What I wanted most of all was to talk to Giles. I would ask him how he managed the emotional part of having cancer. I knew he wouldn't mind the question. But only moments later, I stepped outside to find he was gone. As if he'd simply vanished. I almost wondered if he'd ever really been there at all, or if I had just conjured him out of need.

Was I going crazy, after all? Dick had often implied that, each time I gave in to my deeper fears, responding to tides of emotion and odd notions that were ingrained in me before I ever met him. I went inside to get Rhudy's leash. His puppy love for me was pure, and he didn't care if I was wearing a hospital gown or hadn't washed my hair for days. That lucky, panting, salivating little creature didn't know what cancer was. And I would never have to console him when I was hanging by a thread myself.

Once I had him home, Rhudy seemed especially pleased to snuggle up beside me. I had gotten into bed early, and ate a simple supper of a sandwich on a tray. Downstairs, Dick gazed at the droning TV from his leather chair, as usual. I'd brought my notebook upstairs with me, but I couldn't lose myself in gardening, not tonight. Instead I tossed it toward the nightstand, where it slightly missed, sliding to the floor, with pages splayed. Rhudy lifted his head from Dick's pillow.

My children's pictures stared out sweetly from the shelf. Some were school photos, a couple were professional poses from back in the day when photographers would set up at Kmart or Hills department store. My mind wandered to the times when they were all blond, before darkening to brunette. They were adorable and fun, straight out of central casting. I remembered how I used to rock them to sleep when they were babies.

Not for the first—or last—time, I wondered why on earth my parents hadn't simply let me cry a little more instead of rushing me to some fancy city doctor for the latest treatment.

I thought of Sarah Driscoll's majestic magnolia with its showy flowers. The tree was dazzling, proudly reaching up to the sky, for all the world to see. Looking at it from the outside, the uninformed observer would have no idea that the wood was actually soft and unsuitable for building. In the same way, the cancer diagnosis that left me feeling so vulnerable and weakened wasn't something that could be seen. Even the scar left behind by my lumpectomy was small, insignificant. Looking through the eyes of love, Dick thought I was beautiful, and he told me so often. But the fear I held inside me was something else entirely. I might apply my makeup with a skillful hand or dress to show my figure off, but inwardly, I struggled with a fundamental sense of being flawed. I knew it was horrible and self-defeating to feel this way, but I couldn't help myself. I indulged in terrible fantasies of how easily Dick could restart his life once I was gone.

His first wife—me—had been a real lemon, it turned out, but he'd get luckier the second time around. He'd find someone just as healthy and vital as he was.

These were awful thoughts, and Dick didn't deserve them. But feeling sorry for myself was like rolling down a grassy hill— I picked up speed the more I did it and it got harder to stop.

Dick had offered to go with me for the follow-up ultrasound, but I told him no, he shouldn't even think of it. What I didn't tell him was that I couldn't stand sitting there with his fears as well as my own, feeding off of each other and somehow multiplying. I told him that he shouldn't worry, I could easily ask Sarah or another female friend to go with me. But even as I said that, I knew I would go alone. I didn't want to be the cancer hostess while my friend tried to be reassuring, or while I tried to be positive for her sake. The most I could handle was to sit in that waiting room by myself, arms wrapped around my own torso as if to physically hold myself together.

After that I would stay in hiding for a few weeks, avoiding searching glances and prying questions while I prayed that everything would be okay. I didn't mind telling the details of my medical adventure after a benign result was reached. After the happy ending, it might even be entertaining to admit that while I was outwardly cool I was really a panicky mess. I could joke about fearing the worst and my argument with Dick. I would manage the facts and control my message. Maybe that's what my mother was doing when she had them roll her away in the hearse.

I popped a Xanax and grew drowsy. On the edge of sleep, I

heard Dick's weary footsteps on the stairs. The moon was pale and cold. It peered at me through an opening in the curtains. I threw the covers back and waited in hope for Dick to come lie beside me.

Three days later, feeling dizzy in a little cubicle, I took my sweater off. My bra came next. I hung it on a hook. Heaven help me, I'd avoided wearing pink. Today I chose colors I liked better and that felt more fitting for the occasion—muddy brown and deep gunmetal gray.

One of the nurses stuck her head into my dressing room and said, "Don't forget to get a bumper sticker for the Big Pink Parade. It's for Breast Cancer Awareness month. This year, the mayor is going to speak."

I studied the nurse's expression. She looked sincere. If I were going to think up a parade for breast cancer it certainly wouldn't feature pink. Instead, I would have liked to see a line of scientists in lab coats trooping over distant hills. They would be sexless men and women with their hair cut sensibly, their glasses on and pencils sharpened. And they'd be looking for a cure. I thought of an acquaintance, Dora, who once said she'd kept a positive attitude when she was called back for some further pictures, and she attributed the benign results that came her way to managing her thoughts. The thoughts I managed now were those of bashing Dora's head until her perky voice stopped chirping. That distinctly un-Christian thought aside, I knew I would do anything for this scan to turn out fine, if only God would just cooperate and make it all go away.

The follow-up ultrasound had shown what the mammogram only suggested. There was a lesion, almost certainly malignant. This next scan would show even more, and my Handsome Oncologist had already told me that I was likely facing a double mastectomy. While I waited to be called for the scan, I thought of how I loved my house—the too-small cupboard where I stacked our random coffee cups, the doorknobs that needed polishing, the doorbell that needed fixing, and even the dust that settled on the furniture. *Please,* I prayed, *let it be there for me, all of it, when I return.* I promised not to take for granted any pleasure or annoyance, great or small, that God had granted me in His wisdom and mercy.

Two hours later, my burst of positive prayer was replaced by numbness cultivated in the wake of terror. I stumbled robotically into the parking lot outside the entrance to the radiology department. The sun, a pale white dot, beat down unrelentingly. My throat was scratchy from the Xanax tablets I'd swallowed without regard to proper dosage. The hospital's courtesy golf cart, adorned with a pink bumper sticker, stopped to offer me a ride to my car. Apparently, I looked a little looped.

"Just point me to your car," the elderly driver offered, and he was patient as I thought about my answer for a while. I took the moment to call Dick. Our conversation was brief. He assured me everything would be all right.

I said, "Yes. Of course. Sure."

I fell into a fantasy of leaning forward, pleading with the old man driving the cart to drive faster. I visualized a healthy woman stepping from her car into our path. She managed to escape being hit, but I imagined myself tumbling out, limbs smooth, hair flying free, cartwheeling gracefully to meet my fate. I would die with a look of shock on my face and lipstick intact, ever the aging cheerleader, and a tragic casualty of careless driving only. An administrator high within the building would phone Dick, saying, "She died after a Courageous Battle involving our golf cart shuttle service. You can get on with a normal life now." I saw my helpless parents, confined to bed, being told I was "on vacation for a while." I imagined Rhudy circling his empty water bowl, waiting vainly for my return.

Rumbling down the hill in the golf cart, not at all confident that everything would be all right, I thought of everything I hated about the cancer conversations I was about to set in motion. I heard the phone and doorbell ringing. And I saw the greeting cards with sunsets, rainbows, angels, Jesus, four-leaf clovers, open Bibles, floating clouds, or flower-dotted meadows stretching out with no real end in sight. I knew I should be thankful for the concern that would no doubt follow the news that I had now come to expect. But Lord help me, it all just made me tired.

At home, I waited for Dick to get home from work. I watched him get out of his car, and the effort seemed to exhaust him. At first, he didn't see me, though our front door stood ajar. As he walked along, I caught his eye and there was a hint of courage in the smile he offered, but his eyes were dim and I could have sworn he winced. Another one of my dark thoughts settled over me like a poisonous fog. There were other women in the world. I imagined how they thrust their healthy bosoms toward him, and how their lustrous hairdos rippled suggestively while they munched the secret brand of vitamins effective in preventing things like this.

Yet it was me he wanted, and I knew that. Which somehow made this all the more excruciating. I hated what my body was doing to him—to us.

Inside, we slipped our arms around each other, equally despondent and a perfect fit, as always. But still there was that separation that I couldn't help feeling at times like this. We belonged to two different realms, Dick and I. The well and the sick. The sharp knives were coming out for me, and not for him. I might need chemo as well, but we'd know for sure after surgery.

Ten years ago, on our first reluctant journey through the realm of cellular surprises, we were moved to push some phrases out to cheer ourselves. We would announce to each other: *Things will be okay. We're strong. Hold on. I'll be there.* This time, Dick said that it was okay to be pissed. And then we both embraced silence.

Above us was the lantern where we hung our mistletoe each year. We stood there and held each other, hoping only to get through this moment and the next.

13.

A Pretty Sky

The verdict was in, and a double mastectomy it would be.

Did I cry?

Oh, yes.

I cried alone, before and after greeting Dick.

The bathroom door secured, I pressed a folded washcloth to my face. Coming out, I tried to cultivate a sense of calm. At dinner, Dick admitted that he had a meeting scheduled with a client at his workplace. I insisted he go. Dick had already done me the favor of telling our children the news, because I couldn't bear to do it.

"Truthfully," I told him, "I will be okay. I have some errands. I need a few things from the grocery store."

He held a wary eye on me as he picked up his briefcase, and

we exchanged a chaste kiss. Then I watched him get into his car. A stranger who looked vaguely like Carol greeted me in the mirror as I dabbed the smudges of my eyeliner and traced a tube of lipstick back and forth along my slightly swollen lips.

The mastectomy would take several hours, and then the reconstruction several more. Two surgeons would be involved, one for the mastectomy and a plastic surgeon for the reconstruction. It would be done on a Saturday, when the operating room was available for the entire day. Early in the surgery, they would check the lymph nodes to see if the cancer had spread—a "sentinel node biopsy," they called it, which sounded like something out of *Star Trek*. The first time the surgeon used this term, I felt like saluting. If the nodes were clean, then I wouldn't have to have chemo. If . . .

I couldn't think about that now. Instead, I sat down to make a grocery list. Then I got into my van and drove to Foodland.

I shopped efficiently, my eyes averted, hoping I wouldn't be recognized by anyone in a mood to chat. I didn't even want to see Giles, and I felt relieved when there was no sign of him at the registers.

I rattled out into the parking lot, my groceries rumbling in the cart. A fiery summer sunset purified the sky. The beauty of it struck me like a physical pain, and thoughts of my family flooded me, knocking the wind out of me yet again. I was supposed to be the one who comforted them. How could I bring them hurt like this? Well-meaning friends had urged me to go to a support group when I was first diagnosed, but I'd always resisted it. Now I wondered if I really did need to talk to other women facing the same fears I was. But then I thought, No. One stray remark would send me reeling, and I'd be certain that everyone else's symptoms were signs of things that my own doctors had missed.

Giles's Neon swooped into the lot just as I reached my van. I couldn't deceive him, so instead I tried to avoid him, keeping my head down and planning to jump in and drive away before he could spot me.

But then I noticed how he strode with such joy in the direction of a job he never bargained for. No matter how many disappointments he'd experienced, he never withdrew into a shell of sadness the way I longed to. He kept his face to the sky and his arms open to the world.

So I changed my mind about running away. Right there in the Foodland parking lot where anyone might hear, I went to Giles and poured out my unhappy news. As I talked, his frown grew more pronounced. This was a separate cancer, not a recurrence or metastasis, I explained. "Isn't that a kick? Please say you understand. Do you ever worry that your cancer will come back?"

"Yes. It could. I do."

His eyes were clear, as if he were scanning the horizon for storm clouds. As other shoppers passed us by, he waited for me to say more.

"It's so unfair!" I blurted out, just like a child. His smile was taut, and I barreled on. "Ever since my mother's stroke, I actually began to think I might survive her. I thought she was going to die before the cancer could catch up with me again, and then she wouldn't have to know the pain of burying another child."

Giles shook his head and I sensed disapproval. Desperate to make him understand, I tried again.

"Deep down, Daddy wants me to protect her, just the way I've always done, ever since I was old enough to understand those little pictures in the drawer. But now he's sick and can't express it. My mother, helpless in her bed, can't even ask a question. This time I was supposed to be the healthy one, the caregiver. My life was supposed to make things better for them, not worse. What are we going to do, Giles? I've screwed it all up again!"

Gesturing, I took my hands off the cart, and it rolled into the pathway of a station wagon backing out. Giles rescued it in time. Then he helped me load my bags into the van. "You are not responsible for this disease. It has come to you. You must be well for yourself, and free yourself from this burden you feel. Members of a family wish such health and freedom for each other."

The concept of such freedom was more foreign to me than I could express to Giles. And in a way, it frightened me. I had lived so long weighted down by my belief that I was responsible for my parents' happiness. I wondered if I might just float away, as insubstantial as a feather, if I shed myself of such a central characteristic. Still, I found myself breathing more deeply, my panic quenched by Giles's calm resolve.

Just then, a neighbor, Robert Maxim, passed by wearing shorts and flip-flops. His army T-shirt was wet, as if he'd been washing his car and hadn't stopped to change. "Hello, you guys. A pretty sky, there. Huh?"

Giles and I paused to look at the pink that was dissolving into other rosy shades in the sky. "It is a pretty sky," I answered, hoping to sound interested. Robert nodded and moved on.

I looked back at Giles. "Freedom. It makes perfect sense. I don't know if I can do it, though."

"You have many, many strengths," Giles said.

How I wished—hoped—that were so. Giles made me believe it could be. A lump formed in my throat and I swallowed around it. "Who on earth will I become, beyond this bitterness?"

"Illness comes into each life, but we must not let it define us," Giles said by way of answer. His words were comforting, but I couldn't help noticing that the man who spoke them looked strangely troubled.

The evening before my surgery, I felt a strong need to give Mama and Daddy a final kiss, kind of like tucking children into bed and wishing them sweet dreams. I set out alone to Heathwood Hearth.

I was relieved to discover Mama was already sleeping. Her face was peaceful and her breathing steady. With luck, I wouldn't need chemo and my recovery would be swift enough that I could return to my regular visits in just a few weeks. I placed a hand on the blanket folded underneath her chin and remembered how Judy and I would call to her in the night when we were sick, and how she always came, an angelic presence that instantly made me feel better. Now I tamped down the urge to weep for both of us.

In my father's room, I found the man who used to be Daddy snoring heavily in his recliner. He startled, sensing someone near.

"Dick and I are going on a little trip," I whispered to him, "but I'll be back before you know it. I'll bring you something from our travels. Please listen to the nurses while I'm gone." It disturbed me that I was talking to my father like a child. I knew it was the right thing to keep my new diagnosis from them, but I longed to be the object of comfort instead of the other way around, to be able to put my head in Daddy's lap and have him tell me everything would be okay, that he'd take care of me.

He stared at me, mouth slightly open as if perpetually surprised, and breathing with exaggerated effort.

Okay, I told myself. *We had our moment.* Then I turned to leave. Incredibly, though, as I walked out I heard his soothing voice of old addressing me by name.

"Carol—is there something wrong?" He cleared his throat. "You seem like something's wrong," he forcefully repeated.

His brow gathered in a wrinkle I remembered from my years of growing up. The look was penetrating, and I had a flashback to the man who was impossible to fool, yet easy to adore. His idea of discipline consisted of a big frown, which was used for major offenses, such as telling lies or showing sassy disrespect to him or Mama. There was also the little frown, for minor things such as a ding on the fender of our Dodge Dart Swinger, due to my chatting with a teenage friend and harmonizing with a Beatles' song while driving. I would have sold my soul to stay in favor with this wise and loving man and to keep him looking happy. It was a feeling that had never faded with time, and one that had kept me upright and respectable all through the years.

"Oh, Daddy. Please don't worry." My fingers stroked his forehead. He relaxed by degrees, and it was almost unbearably sad the way he trusted me. His expression softened toward relief, and then contentment.

"*Wabironenore,*" I whispered. Leaving him, I choked back sobs.

In my van, I rested my forehead on the steering wheel. I thought of Giles's advice, allowing grief to overtake me as I wept. The ironies of my life overwhelmed me. My parents had only wanted to help me when they subjected me to those radiation treatments when I was just five months old. But instead, they'd inadvertently planted a dangerous seed inside me. Now I fought with my dueling urge to love and protect them, while also wanting to shake my fist at the universe—and, if I were honest with myself, at them—and ask, *Why me?*

It was the age-old question, a cliché, in fact. Yet sitting alone in my car, I felt neither too holy nor too proud to ask it.

Just after four a.m., Dick drove us to the hospital. A short time later, I lay on a table, prepared for surgery and all alone. I temporarily surrendered to my fate. I had read that giving in like that could be a coping strategy. Or perhaps it was just a recognition of reality—no one is more vulnerable than a patient lying essentially naked on an operating table. What choice is there but surrender?

In any case, I felt a sudden calm. It might have been a gracious helping of the Peace that Passes Understanding. Or maybe it was just the sedative the anesthesiologist had added to my IV.

I prayed, simply at first: *Please let the nodes be clear.*

And then less selfishly: *Please guide Lok, and all of us who entertain our sweet dreams of returning to our families.*

I woke up to no good news being whispered in my ear by Dick.

"Everything went great!" he told me as I was rolled toward my hospital room on the gurney. "You're doing well!"

Still groggy, I couldn't yet press him to be more specific, or to ask him why he hadn't told me the nodes were all clear.

Four hours later, the surgeon visited and I learned the reason for Dick's sidestepping generalities and platitudes. A single node was positive, and that was all it took. I would have to have chemo.

I felt a sadness beyond my power to express to Dick or anyone else. There was a siege just around the corner, and I wasn't at all certain that I had the strength to withstand it.

14.

Potted Plants and
Fresh Flowers

Above the early autumn trees, the sun cast down its slanted
rays, causing the sidewalk where Giles stepped to actually
sparkle. I appreciated the beauty of the blooming realm outside
my window, but it might as well have been a world away from
me. I was hopelessly trapped inside, a prisoner of chemo.

Peering out at Giles from my darkened living room, I thought
about how long it had been since we'd exchanged more than a
hurried word of greeting at the door. He seemed more reserved
than usual these days, but I told myself not to take it personally.
It wasn't easy to figure out the right words to say to me lately.

I'd had two treatments so far, and my counts were in the
tank. Hence my quarantine. Supposedly I was being kept safe

from germs, but I was slowly going mad with the isolation. I was forbidden even to visit my parents, and I tortured myself imagining them like children at camp with their bags all packed but no one to come get them.

I was helpless to change the situation, so instead I sat at my window, like Jimmy Stewart in *Rear Window*, spying on my neighbors.

I watched as Sarah caught up with Giles, her face flushed, her glossy hair held back with sunglasses. They lingered, talking to each other in the animated fashion that was second nature to the walking well. It was something I had taken for granted before, but now I longed for it with a hunger I could taste. Fatigue in all its forms flowed through my veins. Even lifting up my arms to Dick's embrace was an effort, though my weary spirit willed it mightily.

Another neighbor joined the gathering outside. It was Meg, who held her baby in her arms and seemed to have some question that drew all three of them to look back toward her yard.

In the foyer mirror, I inspected my wig. I'd been told it was made of human hair from Europe. It was a tawny color, very thick. With bobby pins to hold some pieces of the bangs back, I imagined it looked vaguely "natural," although the truth was that my face had narrowed in the last few weeks, and my eyes were underscored by two unhealthy stripes of gray. Perhaps it was just as well that I was banished indoors. I could just imagine how my friends would pretend that I looked well, and offer kind compliments that they'd have to struggle to mean.

Everyone had been so nice—supportive and generous, ecstatic that I had another "good prognosis," since my type of cancer was not considered particularly aggressive.

I'd received scores of lovely greeting cards, potted plants, and bouquets of cut flowers. My substitute at school sent along a folder of notes from my students. Our freezer brimmed with casseroles, the kitchen countertops with pies and cakes and plates of cookies, and the phone kept ringing with calls from friends offering to bring us anything we needed.

But I let the calls go to voice mail. As the chemo moved along, Dick and I had been good at keeping up appearances, but the truth was that we were both worn out by the burden. What I needed now was difficult to speak about, and harder still for anyone to comprehend. I needed this metastatic cancer, present in that single node, to tumble back in Time, evolving either into something wholly healthy and benign, or something that had never existed at all—a shadow on a mammogram that turned out to be nothing. My first diagnosis might have turned out well enough, but this second one brought me an inescapable message: *I am cancer and I'm sticking around as long as I can. I've picked you out. You'll never get away.*

Bienta calmly brought her hands together, fingertips just touching. It was a few days later and she took her place behind me at my dressing table. I watched her in the mirror as she pulled a length of pale blue fabric from her knitting bag. The sun was setting, and Dick was at a partners' meeting, so Bienta and I were alone. Dick hadn't wanted me to invite her over. He kept reminding me of my suppressed immunities. I made the illogical argument that since Bienta was a nurse, her germs were safe. Besides, I told him, I was going crazy in the house and my peering through the window at happy people chatting in the street had taken a pathological turn. And I needed Bienta's help. My wig was starting to feel loose and I was afraid of looking truly insane if I tried to walk outdoors with it looking all cockeyed. I wanted Bienta to teach me how to do one of those lovely turbans she sometimes wore to church.

Eyes averted from the mirror, I slid off my wig and settled it on the stiff white Styrofoam. It seemed sort of lordly, or Jeffersonian, resting there. But there was nothing lordly about what I saw in the mirror. I found myself admitting something to Bienta that I couldn't bear to tell Dick. Since the chemo took my hair, I'd started showering at night, without the bathroom light on.

"Oh?"

"Please don't tell Dick. He doesn't know."

"I see." She answered quickly, but her tone held neither shock nor condemnation. Something in the guarded way she managed her facial expression without betraying what she really felt struck me as utterly familiar. I recognized myself in how she pressed on, intent, it seemed, on keeping all the promises she'd ever made.

Through the bedroom window, I saw the moon, a floating

presence in the deeply purple sky. I sighed. "My favorite time of day," I readily confessed.

"It is?"

"Darkness is my friend," I offered, heartened by her interest and the cozy wraparound of nighttime in the offing. "It helps in my campaign to minimize my glimpses of the nakedness up here." I pressed my palm to my scalp. It felt alien, rubbery. "Also, I imagine I see cancer everywhere on my body. I check moles or lumps or bumps. I notice splotches, rashes, blood from any orifice. Also, I check for indentations, any pouching-out or puckering. Wheezy breathing, headaches, indigestion, and various old scars make the imaginary list as well. I can't turn it off, Bienta. So I turn the lights off instead. At least that switch is something I control."

I braced myself. I assumed Bienta would tell me that I needed a counselor. I'd already covered that base, though. I had a good therapist, and I saw her every week. But what I also truly needed was friendship from a woman who wasn't frightened by my veering from the script. I just couldn't pretend to be a good sport all the time while managed doses of poison were dripped into my body—a body I no longer recognized. I just wasn't one of those women who embraced wearing pink as a symbol of pride and solidarity, and went around bald with a flower painted on her head.

I didn't think Bienta would expect that of me, though. And I also instinctively felt that she'd never betray my confidence. I had dear friends in town, but there was no one I could be absolutely certain wouldn't share my fears with someone else. And they wouldn't do it out of spite—it would be out of concern and a desire to help. But I couldn't bear that. This town was just too small. Once, I remembered passing a young woman on the street and it amazed me that I didn't remember her name, but I did vividly recall being told that her first baby was born breech. Far be it from me to judge anyone else on that score, but I was determined not to be the subject of conversation.

"Yes. I understand," Bienta said, after a few moments of careful thought. "We do strange things when we're in hiding. And in Africa, you would find many people who bathe at night, in lakes or rivers, in the moonlight, seeking privacy. An indoor bathroom is a luxury."

"But what about the hippos? Aren't they dangerous?" I recalled Giles saying something about hippos in one of his stories about growing up.

"Oh, they will kill you for the sport of it," she said mildly. "Quite true. One must be careful." It struck me how much more comfortable—or perhaps "accustomed" was the better word—Giles and Bienta were with danger and with death.

Bienta's dark brown eyes met mine. The colors of our eyes were a perfect match. I watched the skill with which Bienta wrapped her pretty fabric to transform my nakedness. In the mirror, I looked flirty, feminine, even mysterious.

"You're just as gifted as my plastic surgeon," I said.

"Do you still go back to him?"

"He adds a little sterile water to expand the implants, week by week. As soon as my breasts are as big as I want them to be, he'll put in the permanent implants. It's another surgery. Maybe in the spring." It was strange to be talking this way about such an intimate part of my body, but Bienta's calm matter-of-factness took away any shame or embarrassment I might have felt.

"And are you happy with the result so far?"

That was a difficult question to answer. Even though I thought they looked very good in a sort of abstract way, they didn't feel real to me. I'd been warned that I might never regain as much sensitivity as I'd once had, but I wasn't prepared for the profound lack of sensation. I could have walked down the street with my shirt accidentally unbuttoned and I wouldn't even have felt a warning breeze. And although I'd been rather small-chested before and now I could size up if I wanted to, I'd always liked my breasts the way they were.

"I'm kind of afraid to look at them," I admitted to Bienta. "I'm afraid to enjoy them, because I can't stop worrying that another tumor is going to pop up. I had a scare a few weeks ago, because I thought I felt something, and it turned out to be just a suture. So I sort of feel like I'm wearing two time bombs on my chest. And if they don't go off, then, well, I guess they look really good."

The sky grew darker yet. Bienta quietly took in everything I said, and there was something soothing about the way she wrapped my head with her lengths of lovely cloth. My breasts didn't feel like quite my own, but at least now I wasn't wearing some stranger's hair. "I used to feel a certain freedom in existing," I said, while studying the way Bienta's able fingers pressed and tucked the fabric. "Is it so wrong to search for that again? Do you think I'm crazy? Please tell the truth."

"Hardly, Mrs. Wall. Have I ever told you how I met my husband?" she abruptly asked.

"You haven't. No."

"It was at Egerton College. Owita sat on a low wall as I arrived with luggage, and he asked a friend to introduce us. I was from the city, Nairobi. He had arrived, the bright, successful son of the community of proud Rusinga and a member of our Luo tribe."

"So, then, he helped you with your luggage . . ."

"Yes."

"And was it love at first sight?"

"There was an interest on both sides," she admitted, with a sly look. I laughed out loud. "My father was devout, and Giles was baptized just before we married."

"I converted shortly after my marriage," I said. "The town of Radford thought we'd lost our minds! We were so young, and they had never heard of such a thing. He was nineteen, and I was twenty—still in college."

"But your parents gave their blessing?"

"Yes. We couldn't bear to be apart, and they took pity on us. Or . . . they saw . . ." I hesitated. "They saw," I started to say again. "I think they must have somehow seen our happy future. In their wisdom. I'll just leave it there." I plucked a tissue to wipe the dampness in my eyes.

"We've been arguing a lot, these days, Bienta." I snatched another tissue from its plastic holder and took a moment to compose myself before continuing. "I even told him I hated him. How could I say a thing like that? Dick has stood by me, through all these trials, yet a person has his limits. Don't you think? What if my husband, being human, might seek out consolation with another woman who is more appealing, even younger, perhaps? He could have more children with this newer, fresher, younger wife. Life could start over for him."

Bienta turned her head slightly but held her gaze on me. "Are these your ideas or his?"

"Last night I dreamed I was waiting for a train. I felt such joy as the train approached my station, and I watched in horror as it passed me by without even slowing down."

"That sounds more like a nightmare," Bienta said.

I fought back tears as I told the rest. "Now and then, through the window of the speeding train, I caught a glimpse of Dick in the dining car, with a person I couldn't see. I imagined the twilight consuming him, and I wondered if he'd miss me half as much as I'd miss him."

"So, would she have to be perfect?" Bienta said.

"Yes."

"How do you define perfect?" she asked.

I answered without hesitation. "Someone who could provide a normal mammogram certified by the Mayo Clinic and could pack the perfect suitcase, striding off on ballet-dancer legs to meet him at the airport for the perfect getaway!"

"The perfect suitcase? What does it contain?" I was surprised to see the mischief in her smile.

"Several negligees and one good suit from Talbots," I impulsively replied. Then we both collapsed in laughter. It was a delicious feeling, being able to admit my darkest fears out loud—and knowing that losing Dick, my lover and best friend, was far more terrible to me than having cancer. Maybe there was some power in realizing that cancer wasn't actually the worst thing that could happen to me.

An hour later, Dick arrived home. He complimented me on the head wrap.

"You're feeling better, aren't you?" he ventured casually, while leafing through the mail.

"Yes. I think I am."

I didn't tell him that when Bienta left a short time earlier I stood before the bathroom mirror for a good long time, studying the angles of my face, and applying makeup with a heavy hand, as if it were prom night or my wedding day. I wasn't sure which.

Just then, Giles rang our doorbell, handing Dick a potted plant for me and saying he couldn't come in because the boys were waiting in the car. Rushing to Dick's side to greet Giles, I quickly scanned the get-well card. Looking at the handwriting, I realized that Giles had signed Bienta's name beside his own. Something in this minor detail captured my attention. He admired my head wrap, and was surprised to know it was Bienta who had assisted me.

"You mean she didn't tell you she was coming here today?" I said.

Giles answered no, while stepping back onto the porch. "I've had a cold," he said, by way of awkward explanation.

I started to follow him out to his car, but Dick held me back with a protective arm. I'd taken enough chances with my suppressed immunities for one day.

Inside, I held the curtain back to watch as Giles drove off. The boys were in the car, but not Bienta. More and more, it struck me how this bright, accomplished, and attractive couple traveled in the same circles but never really seemed to be together.

SEPT. 12

Dear Giles & Bienta,

The snake plant (S. trifasciata laurentii, I should say) is absolutely wonderful. I cleared a place for it on our mantel, where the architectural beauty of the blade-like leaves can be appreciated more fully. Surely when you selected it you had my "gift" for growing things in mind, as the information card says it's among the toughest of houseplants and can only be killed by either overwatering or by not watering at all. I will try my very best to do neither. Let's all keep our fingers crossed, regarding that.

The chiseled, upright leaves somehow remind me of my good prognosis, so we celebrate together, even in the midst of challenges. Bienta, I meant to point out yesterday that my choir chair will be empty for a while. You would be more welcome than you know, and easily could bring me some reports on things, from time to time. Just before I dashed away for surgery, Mike, our director, was considering Handel's "He Shall Feed His Flock" for Advent. Knowing how you like the Crimond "Lord's My Shepherd," I suspect this might also be a favorite of yours. In any case, believe me when I say that your soprano notes are needed.

Lastly, I ventured out for a drive with Dick last night, my head wrap intact and the rest of my outfit chosen to accentuate the pretty azure blue of the fabric, that is, conveniently, blue jeans and a white blouse. We stopped in front of Sarah's house, where she and Henry came out to admire your handiwork. We were all agreed that it is definitely my best "look," for the season, though I will wear the wig from time to time, as well.

I continue to pray for Lok. Please let me know of any news.

Erokamano, and with gratitude (redundantly),

Carol Wall

SEPT. 13

Dear Mrs. Wall,

Bienta and I appreciate your kind note. Please feel free to consult me in the event of any untoward developments regarding the snake plant, a succulent which grows very tall in our native country and with which I am well acquainted.

As for the information you had earlier requested:

—pumpkins, butternut and acorn squash, all gourds, are high in beta-carotene (Vitamin A . . . useful in fighting infections)

—the pumpkins I installed by the fence should be harvested 2–3 weeks after they have turned orange, but before the first light frost, at which time they will be physiologically mature. They are not quite ready yet.

—Mrs. Driscoll and I will be happy to create a fall display: pumpkins and other gourds, with bales of hay, just as you requested, to greet your family members as they return to your compound to check on your progress.

Lastly, Bienta has asked me to say that we appreciate, as always, your faithfulness in praying for our dear Lok. We have been speaking to an official at the embassy in Nairobi, so are very hopeful of a favorable outcome soon.

Sincerely,

Giles Owita

[WRITTEN FROM CHEMO LAB]

APRIL 4

Dear Giles,

I'm sorry not to have written you sooner, but my thinking is a little cloudy these days. I can't believe how long I've been *kept from speaking to you in person. Has it really been eight long months? But with my counts still low, my "jailer"—Dick— remains determined to keep me inside. I guess you heard that, following a previous treatment, I had to have a needle stick and got phlebitis, thus returning to the hospital for several days. I'm perfectly fine, I'll add, having also weathered some problems with one of my incisions, which now, via a bit of minor surgery, has been resolved. These complications have kept me indoors even more than I had anticipated, and I do regret my long absence from friends and neighbors, not to mention my students at St. B's. I do hope the boys like going to school there.*

Visits to my parents are still forbidden to me at this time, which has been a terrible source of worry and guilt for me. If you could say a prayer for them, I would be grateful. My mother possibly has had another minor stroke. We all think that Mama wonders where I am. She is unable to say this, but seems agitated about something. For now, we are telling her I've gone out of town, and will see her soon. As for Daddy, pray the Lord will keep him out of trouble, anchored by some sense, however dim, of knowing he is deeply, deeply loved.

I pledge continuing my nightly prayers for Lok. Prayer is the most powerful thing I can do right now. How eagerly you must all await a resolution! I also pray the boys continue their St. Benedict successes. They can help me catch up on the gossip later in the spring when I return.

My bag of chemo drip is almost empty, and we all have so

many miles to go before we sleep. Just please remember I appreciate your kindness at this time.

Your friend (osiepi),
Carol Wall

Dear Mrs. Wall,

Enclosed please find the bill requested by Mr. Wall.

Bienta and I rejoice to hear your chemotherapy is almost at an end. You are missed in your yard and in the neighborhood, at school and church, as well. Yet we know that your confinement and your trials have come in the best interest of your future health, so we are patient.

All on the street are inquiring. Mrs. Driscoll has given us reports of your telephone conversations and brief visits. Today, she sends you the message that she's expecting further issues with her beautiful gardenias and those aphids that may very well settle in again. She is going to try some lady beetles, which will eat the aphids. If you have suggestions, she is completely open and exasperated, she reports. Mr. Robert Maxim has announced his engagement to the niece of a local woman. A garden wedding is set for late July, at Mr. Maxim's home, and he requests I ask you to assist Mrs. Driscoll and me in the planning of a trellis that can function as a focal point. Further up the street, the Saunders lady sends you word of copious amounts of golden squash she will be planting and will send your way. She will leave it on your porch, starting later in the season. The widow lady on the corner contemplates a sunflower to celebrate your courage, and she anticipates a time when you and she will stand together in her yard, admiring it.

At every house along the street, you have a neighbor who is listening and waiting. Bienta often says that all of us would fare a little better if we cultivated our connections with the ones around us, and her words are always wise. Any news of your improvement adds a note of cheer as I go up and down the sidewalk. I am pleased to say that Lok received the ruby-colored rose you pressed last year, before this current trouble started, between the pages of your heavy classroom dictionary. I sent it shortly after you gave it to me, but the mail is slow in coming. It finally arrived. She has placed it in her Luo Testament, and she thanks you very, very much.

Bienta said your name was recently included in the Prayers of the Faithful, during Mass. She urged that I go with her last week, and I did, standing to the side as she lit a candle on behalf of all your needs and the dilemmas of your People.

I do believe her prayers go quickly up. The Saints of God are well acquainted with my wife. If I am sure of anything, I'm sure of this.

Your friend,
Giles Owita

15.

Green Plants, Only

My feelings were mixed as I rang the bell to mark the end of my chemo. My Handsome Oncologist had told me I might feel that way, although I hadn't believed him until this moment. For nine long months, I had been tethered to the chemo lab with its toxic brew of hopefully helpful chemicals administered by a caring and very talented staff. In other words, I had been doing something positive to fight potential cancer cells that might remain—and a lot of spiffy people had supported me and given me top-notch care.

Now I was on my own again. It felt like a free fall.

Dick was at my elbow as we walked away. We waved off the golf cart shuttle and Dick volunteered to pull the van up for me.

But I said no, and I matched him, stride for stride across the parking lot, my shadow narrow and thin beside his larger, more proportioned one. I wondered if he felt a little empty, just as I did.

Arriving home, we saw Giles pacing at the line of boxwoods in our yard. Intent on his inspection, he did not look up until we pulled into the driveway.

"Eh!" he called to both of us.

"This is it!" I cheerfully announced with my hands flung wide. "And in a few more days, when my blood counts have risen a bit, I can start assisting you again."

"Every day brings something good!" Giles answered with his trademark ease, his accent heavy, just as always, on the final consonant.

"I'm going to learn a lot, this time," I said. "More hands-on stuff. Okay?"

"This yard is ready for you, Mrs. Wall." He flashed his million-dollar smile. "Many of my projects will require your assistance. I have some new ideas for us, as well."

I saw a small white book protruding from the back pocket of his navy work suit.

"What's that?" I said.

Reaching toward it, he became more sober. "Bienta sent this. She said she hoped that it would help to answer some of your questions. I believe you spoke to her about your mother? How is she faring, Mrs. Wall?"

"I haven't seen her since that night I tucked them into bed, nine long months ago. I'm going there next week. Poor Dick has managed all of us. Can you believe it?"

Giles shook his head and made a sympathetic clucking sound. I suddenly thought of Lok and felt a pang of guilt for dwelling on my lengthy separation from my parents while Giles and Bienta's situation was so much worse. Yet we all had our sadness, as Giles himself would have said to me, and I had to learn to stop comparing the shares we were each given.

Inside, I opened the small white book and found a letter tucked inside.

APRIL 26

Dear Mrs. Wall,

Thank you for your questions. I found this book among my things, and loan it in the hope that certain passages noted below might be useful.

Recall our discussion about your mother's difficulty with the spoken word. Hers is an especially challenging case, as she cannot ask questions nor reliably express herself. In addition, she may display emotions that are not appropriate to the situation, so you should not expect too much from the reunion. Most of all, you should not take things personally should she cry out or otherwise appear to be upset with you. As to the specific question asked in our recent phone conversation, she is probably not aware of how much time has passed since she saw you last. I will add here, however, that your dilemma touches my heart to an extent I cannot adequately express. You and your People continue in my prayers. You and your husband have weathered things admirably. Not everyone could do that.

In general, I would say that your mother would not be alarmed were you to decide to wear your wig instead of appearing with either the head wrap or the very short hair which you describe. If she is able, and if her vision is intact, she may well note a difference, but I feel that she will focus on the joy of seeing you again, these many months having passed, and will not be inclined to wonder if you have been under treatment for cancer.

In any case, do not carry regret of any kind into your reunion with your parents. Simply let the joy of this precious moment in Time be yours, just as you will do in your joyous and long-awaited return to your students. The substitute has been adequate, my spies report. But for many months, your students have longed to hear your voice and enjoy the amusing things you say. Your ways are fair. You are loved at Saint B's.

We will all pray that you and your dear parents continue to receive the Lord's healing grace.

Blessings,

Bienta Owita

Perhaps Mama was waiting for me, and that's what kept her holding on to life. I had told Daddy that I was going on a trip, and it turned out to be a longer absence than any of us had expected.

But she waited for me before she said goodbye, and for that I was grateful.

Dear Bienta,

Thank you for loaning me this very helpful text. Your wise counsel helped me make the last few weeks of my mother's life a time of comfort and spiritual healing for her. She died at peace.

You were right about the wig. I wore it, and she never seemed to question things, although she did reach out a time or two as if to tug at it. Thank goodness, I was faster, dodging away from her hand to prevent an "unveiling."

Please also express my thanks to Giles for giving me the excellent suggestions for the casket topper. I'll be meeting with the florist later today, in Radford. I will think of you both on Friday as we carry forth the theme of "For the Beauty of the Earth," my mother's favorite hymn. I should add that during these last weeks with her, it seemed she especially enjoyed any story of Giles's ongoing work in my yard. I had to embellish a bit because of my long winter of being indisposed and out of touch. As I wove these tales, my mother's eyes were closed, but a pleasant look would sometimes brighten her face. I only regret that she did not have the opportunity to meet you. She has always been an admirer of "quality people," and I feel that one of the greatest gifts she has given me is the ability to recognize them for myself.

With a heart full of gratitude,

Carol Wall

I stood beside my mother's open grave, a hand pressed more than lightly to my head as breezes blew. I wore the wig, a final token of respect for Mama, in case she was looking down and hadn't had her briefing on my second cancer saga yet.

The time that I'd been dreading all my life was here. The funeral canopy snapped and fluttered as my childhood's darkest fear sank in. Mama had passed away. Her body joined Barbara's in the ground.

I was pleased with the way the casket topper featured the various greens of leaves, velvety-looking moss, and the single Easter lily that celebrated the role of faith in my mother's earthly journey.

She used to take us out on nature walks when we were little. Each of us had a little paper bag for collecting acorns, folds of lime-green moss, leaves displaying shapes and forms to stir the imagination. I visualized the notebook page containing Giles's suggestions for Mama's casket topper, written in his bold, distinctive script. "Leaves of the hosta," I recalled him writing as I held the notebook steady on the railing of the porch.

"Green plants, only," I had requested. "Natural things were what she loved and what she led us to discover on our walks."

"Fern and weeping willow, lamb's ear," Giles continued. "Lime-green mosses, if selected carefully." Once he'd finished his list, he looked in my direction. "These nature walks, perhaps, are part of why you favor greener hues to highly colored, cultivated blossoms?"

"Maybe, Giles. I've never thought of that." It was certainly a positive way of looking at my aversion to flowers.

My children had left the cemetery now. Each one was given a creamy-white, long-stemmed rose to place on their grandmother's casket, on top of the greenery. A few feet away was Barbara's headstone, where her birth and death dates hovered close together, pointing to the heartache that no Kodak print could ever capture. From my vantage point, I looked out across the rolling hills of Radford, remembering all the times Daddy had taken me here to place flowers on her grave.

Thunder rumbled as I noted the roofs of newer houses among the crowded treetops. Wasn't there a cave we used to climb around in, somewhere over there? Now that I was a parent, life seemed much more dangerous, the risks I took a little shocking. In the distance, I saw the outlines of the high school Dick and I attended, now with extra wings, a brand-new gym, a soccer field that was fashioned out of a landscape that was once dust, tall grass, and scrub pines.

Driving into town today, we passed by Daddy's old hotel. The newsstand and bookstore he operated for many years had been converted into a sandwich shop. He didn't even recognize the street, and he spoke to Mama as if she were there. "Margaret, look how blue the sky is! Not a cloud in sight!"

My fingertips caressed the fern that trembled on the casket. I was finding it hard to leave Mama here.

Dick helped Daddy into the car, which was parked downhill.

I watched my father fold his lanky legs into the vehicle, cooperating stiffly, with his glance a dimly executed exercise in random caution. Poor thing, even after viewing Mama in her coffin, he had been puzzled as to what we were doing here. Over and over today, despite our repeated explanations, he'd said, "Girls, I've got to find your mother!"

Maybe we shouldn't have brought him. Just last week, Dick got a phone call from the Roanoke police, who'd found Daddy wandering in town, not far from heavy traffic. He wouldn't be returning to Heathwood Hearth after this. Judy had found him a more secure facility closer to her.

Thunder rumbled again, and the trees shivered, oaks and maples shedding their leaves reluctantly. Evergreens that formed a border for the cemetery made me think of wildly swaying hula skirts. I held my wig in place more tightly.

We were safely in the car as heavy raindrops started their slide along the windshield and more thunder sounded. Rivulets of water streamed down the canvas canopy over Mama's grave. I remembered Mama kneeling to tie on my winter cap or help me button up my raincoat in weather like this. Now, incredibly, it seemed we were going to leave her here in this terrible downpour, as well as for all the weather that came after that.

It was comforting to think of my mother and Barbara, together at last. I didn't claim to be an expert on heaven, but I believed that's how it worked.

The wind picked up even more. I looked out through the watery scrim of raindrops on the car window. The workers stood away from the gravesite, their eyes downcast respectfully. One worker sat on the heavy digging equipment in the background, poised to complete his assignment once we'd left the cemetery.

None of us seemed in a hurry to leave and we made small talk. Finally, I was the one to say, "What are you waiting for, Dick?"

As Dick drove, I had a vision of my mother—it couldn't have been a memory, and yet it felt just that sharp and real. She wore a pink-and-brown gingham housedress, strappy sandals, and anklets, and she held Barbara against her hip. Mama's bangs were cut in a Mamie Eisenhower style, and a little black-and-white beagle we used to have—his name was Crisco—leaped into the plastic backyard swimming pool. Barbara leaned toward our mother smiling, and Mama smiled back.

16.

Impatiens

My cell phone almost never rang when I was at school. But just after lunch, I heard it bleating from the bottom of my purse.

As I fished it out, I heard the new boy, Sam, reading his favorite quote from *Our Town*. Each student in the class was supposed to pick one, and then give a presentation about how it related to the overall theme of the play. Sam delivered his chosen lines well.

"Hello?" I whispered into my phone.

It was Sarah. "Carol? Oh, I'm sorry to disturb you, but . . ." Her voice was shaky. She was usually so steady.

"What's wrong?" I said.

"Giles has had a stroke." She struggled to control her emotions. "It's serious. He collapsed at home. Paralysis. Loss of language skills. They're still assessing."

I sat down in an empty student desk. Just like Mama. Only two months ago, Giles had helped me with her casket topper.

"Mrs. Wall, are you all right?" A thoughtful girl named Maggie touched my arm.

"Yes. Fine. Just tired," I said.

My gaze found the narrow bank of windows at the back of my classroom. Cars and trucks raced by on the expressway. They moved too quickly, weaving in and out. Why must they be in such a hurry? The outside world seemed unreal. We were having a perfectly good day, and then . . .

I heard Sam's voice reciting his lines. "Do any human beings ever realize life while they live it?—every, every minute?"

After school that day, I sat at home awaiting word on Giles. Unable to concentrate on anything else, I stared out at the yard. Everywhere I looked, Giles's handiwork was evident, and simple to identify. Whatever looked especially beautiful had been nurtured by his hand these past three years.

Sarah phoned to ask if I had heard anything from Bienta.

"That's what I was going to ask you," I said.

"We've heard nothing more," she said. "Listen. I've got a high-maintenance client on Wildwood Mountain who wants some plants delivered in time for a party tonight. Why don't you come along with me? I'd love the company and I could use the extra pair of hands. Plus, this client adores Giles and I dread telling her. She'll be so upset."

I agreed to go with her. It would be better than sitting here by myself, stewing.

When she arrived, Sarah's van was stuffed to the gills with ferns and hanging baskets of red geraniums. We pretended to be cheery, but lapsed into quiet for most of the drive. I thought of how many people depended on Giles, of Bienta and the children, and especially of Lok, who was an ocean away. I was terrified for them—and for him.

Sarah steered the Shoppe van up a winding drive that led us through a riotous display of wild dogwood, scrub pines, and a scattering of mountain laurel. "The Blue Hills Mansion is the last house on Wildwood Drive. Have you ever been inside?"

"No," I said, "but I've seen pictures in the newspaper. I hear it's quite the showplace."

"That's our client. She's lived there for forty years, and wants things just so."

We passed several other stately homes, all built in the railroad boom of the early 1900s, all made of the same dark brick, and featuring expansive covered porches. We reached the top and parked in the driveway of the Blue Hills Mansion. I watched from the van as Sarah rang the doorbell and a well-dressed woman with a helmet of lacquered white hair answered. A younger woman, possibly her daughter, came out, too.

I couldn't help noticing the sleekness of the younger girl's figure and the Hollywood perfection of her healthy, flowing hair.

There was a time, not very long ago, when I would have identified more with the daughter than the mother. I would have looked at the younger woman through narrowed eyes, wondering how I compared, and most likely overcome with envy. But I had undergone a slow transformation over the last year. I had come to a gradual acceptance that I was "that lady"—the one who drove slower than all the impatient younger folks on the highway, the one who younger men found invisible, and who reminded younger women of their mothers. But instead of resenting that shift, I decided to embrace it. In our youth- and health-obsessed culture, it was either win or lose, and I decided not to play that game at all. The contest was rigged anyway—because everyone, sooner or later, was going to age out of the running. So I decided to just get over myself. The world would not end if I had a bad hair day or didn't monitor every bite of food that went in my mouth.

This young girl in the bloom of youth was not my enemy, and I was just happy to be alive and to have some hair. Though it was only a few inches long, it was beginning to have some style potential.

As Sarah and I unloaded the plants and arranged them as instructed by the lady of the house, I allowed myself a moment of optimism. If I could get well, then surely Giles could also. It would only be fair.

When some days later Bienta called me with an update, she was subdued. She offered few details about Giles's status, and I was cautious with my questions, knowing how protective I had felt of my mother in those early days. She told me that a family friend named Blake had offered to coordinate communications, so I would be hearing from him.

Blake called that very evening, saying that Giles had been moved to a room on the sixth floor of the hospital. He was scheduled for speech and physical therapy, starting right away. At this point, visiting was very much discouraged, Blake informed me.

"Have you seen him?"

"Yes," he answered carefully. "He's through the worst of it, I think, but isn't saying much of anything. It's early, the speech pathologist has said."

After I hung up with Blake, I mulled over his words. A rule-follower by nature, I took myself by surprise when I decided to ignore his admonition not to visit. I simply decided, wrong or right, that I must be a notable exception to that rule.

The next day, I eased my van along the narrow road that took me by the river, toward the hospital. I stopped my van to snap the parking ticket from its metal slot, recalling how Dick and I drove through this very place the morning of my surgery, almost a year ago, a mingling of fear and hope sustaining us. The course we followed through this concrete, belly-of-the-beast garage was too familiar to me now.

At room 605, I placed my hand against the door and gave a gentle push. A small sign reminded me, "No Visitors," but I ignored it. The door fell open and a slice of light illuminated a bed.

There was Giles's unmoving body, covered completely by tight-stretched sheets. Another sheet was draped over his head. I felt all the dread and horror that I now associated with hospitals. My hand went to my throat protectively.

A nurse came in and whispered to me, "He won't communicate. Everyone has given it their best, but he is taking no food, drink, or pills. Do you know him well?"

"You could say that." I raised my voice. "Giles Owita, this is the worst gardening student you have ever had."

There was no answer, and I feared two things at once—that he couldn't understand me and that he'd slipped away from all of us. So I prayed. *Oh please, God, don't tell me he has died.* I called his name again, "Giles."

He brought one hand up into the air, fingers curled. He grasped the sheet and pulled it off his face. "Eh!"

He was thinner and more frail than I'd expected, but relief washed over me when he greeted me with his dawning smile, however dim.

The nurse leaned toward me and said softly, "Do you mind if I stay and take some notes on your conversation? He hasn't spoken for several days."

"You're kidding. This is the friendliest person I have ever known," I said. "Of course that's okay. Have a seat over there. This man has a Ph.D. in horticulture. Maybe he's just been in shock because of the pitiful condition of some of the plants around here."

The nurse laughed and Giles smiled.

I looked back at Giles. The fingers of his right hand fluttered slightly. In my memory, I saw them healing my azaleas.

"How are you doing?" I said.

He tried to speak, but only garbled syllables came out. His voice was rusty, as if all it needed were exercise. When I softly grasped his nearer hand, it was limp and lifeless, just as Mama's had been. I remembered her futile efforts at communication and her anger.

"Just listen to me," I said to Giles. "You will be stronger, and we'll stand beside the creek again. I need some sound advice on subdividing because my yard is overflowing with so many things, like ornamental grasses and a thousand vibrant blossoms, thanks to everything you've done."

His eyes were eager and he pushed out more syllables, yet none of them made sense. I pretended to understand, although it was difficult to overcome the growing awkwardness I felt. This brilliant man was fluent in so many languages and yet now he was rendered speechless. I wanted to cry.

Suddenly, I felt another presence in the room. My suspicion was confirmed when Giles looked quickly to the left of me. I turned around to see Bienta standing in the doorway. She, too, looked exhausted.

"Oh, Bienta!" I exclaimed.

I walked toward her, offering a hug, and she seemed pleased.

"I hope I'm not intruding. Remember how you helped me when Mama had her stroke? I wanted to be a friend to you, the way you've been to me."

There was a beat of silence. I wondered if she truly thought of me that way.

Giles tried his best to speak. What came out was more gibberish. But then I was astonished when a look of joy transformed Bienta's face.

"Did you not know that Giles is speaking to you, very clearly, in Swahili? His voice was strong! I heard it, coming down the corridor. Now he's telling you even more."

I looked to Giles, who blinked a few times—in relief, it seemed.

"He's concerned about those 'things.' He says he cannot remember the names of them. The ones he planted by your fence, out back," Bienta translated.

"You mean the white impatiens?"

"Those," Giles said in English, as his fingers fluttered at the sheet.

Bienta spoke to him in Luo. I recognized its cadence in the clean economy of phrasing, and I saw Giles nod, confirming certain phrases.

"He wanted to tell you it's a little sunny, where he planted them, and so . . ." Bienta trailed off.

"A dose of water wouldn't hurt," I finished for us all.

Giles smiled, a look of satisfaction relaxing his features and quieting his fluttering hand.

"These are the first sensible words he's spoken to anyone in any language whatsoever," Bienta said softly. "Thank you, Mrs. Wall. For being his friend."

I searched her face. Emotion threatened my composure and I struggled to hold myself steady. It wouldn't do to break down in front of two such strong people who had withstood so much.

"Lok will call tonight," she said to Giles, in English. "Mrs. Wall has given us good news to tell her."

I patted Giles's left hand and told him that I would continue my prayers for healing.

Then I turned to make a quiet departure.

I could hear Bienta's voice as I walked away, speaking again in Luo, the language of their younger days.

17.

Gardening Seminars

The bell rang for dismissal, and in less than thirty seconds, I was alone. Every teacher lives for that moment.

An early-turning apple tree swayed in the September breeze. I admired its sturdy branches through my classroom window. Peering through the burnished canopy of leaves, I saw houses near the airport many blocks away. In one of them resided my friend and favorite gardener. It had been a year since his stroke, and I visited him often. His gait remained unsteady, even with a cane, but the liveliness in his speech patterns was slowly returning.

I crossed the empty classroom to retrieve my marble gardening notebook from the desk drawer. Sitting down, I flipped the pages, trying to find the notes I'd made on the first of our

"gardening seminars"—which is what I had come to call our visits. I remembered the way I had stepped cautiously across the
tilted wooden slats of the ramp that had been installed for Giles's
wheelchair. Arriving at the door, I heard his rusty-sounding
voice call out through the screen:

"Eh! *Amosi!* Come on in!"

I'd been worried about what I might see when I opened the
door. Giles's health insurance had cut off his physical therapy
abruptly, and we all worried that it was too soon, that Giles was
far from restored to health. But that day I was surprised to find
Giles sitting in his wheelchair with his smile restored. He wore
a zip-up nylon running suit. Some sort of college text lay open
on the TV tray in front of him. Still, despite his liveliness, I
couldn't help noticing that his legs seemed thin, and his knees
too prominent.

"Please sit," he had offered, pointing to a chair across from
him, as I pulled the marble notebook from my purse.

"You have brought . . ." he said, a pointer finger spinning in
the air, in my direction. "Your notebook!" he at last confirmed,
his expression brighter for the modest triumph of a successful
word retrieval.

"Here is where you wrote the notes when Mama passed
away." I showed him. "Now we're starting on a brand-new section. Every yard must have its flowers," I reminded him.

"Exactly right," he answered, open to the plan. "I see my
student has been studying."

Since that first seminar months ago, Giles had put on needed weight and there was new enthusiasm in his voice each time I saw him. And each time, he gave me new tasks to perform. September was to be a busy month:

Week of September 14—Mount Vernon Road—1. divide irises, transplanting some to fence line.

Week of September 21—same location . . . deadheading of roses/ pruning of rosebushes. Height to be reduced by one-half to two-thirds to prevent swaying in winter breezes, which can lead to breakage.

I closed the notebook, grabbed my purse, and raced to my van in the faculty parking lot. I had a laundry list of errands to run, but visiting Giles was first on the list. My other tasks would have to wait. Still, I was conscious of feeling rushed and impatient.

I brought my hustle and bustle into Giles's house with me. Giles was quiet, and I asked after Bienta and the boys as I always did.

"The boys are on a soccer trip," he said.

"That's right. They left from school."

"They did," he said. "I hope they win. They've worked so hard."

"They have."

Giles definitely didn't seem himself. Perhaps, I thought, he just wasn't up for a visit today. "Are you okay?" I said. "You look stressed."

"Oh, we are fine," he quickly answered. "There are just a few things which have gone awry."

"Awry? What do you mean?" I asked the question, but no

answer came. I should have pressed him. I should have forgotten my errands and attended to my friend with due respect, an open mind, and my listening skills tuned to the maximum. Instead, I took the easier course. I rushed out, and continued with my errands.

The following Monday, I came home from school to find a voice mail.

Giles's voice was strong, his message blunt.

"Mrs. Wall . . . this is Giles Owita. They are going to cut our water off today. Bienta doesn't know that I am contacting you. Thank you very much."

Speeding as I drove to Giles's house, I pondered weighty questions. Why was I such an idiot? How difficult were certain things to calculate?

Instead of fussing over garden plans, I should have made a column in my notebook for the steady stream of medical expenses that always flowed in the wake of something serious, especially with intensive care involved.

Giles had health insurance. That was why he took the Foodland job in the first place. But even after the insurance had paid its portion, overwhelming amounts remained. Just a fraction of a bill like that would have been too much for any family. A few dollars here and there and some casseroles delivered by concerned friends weren't even a scratch on the surface of all that debt.

I wished we had all thought of it sooner, but recrimination wouldn't help Giles and Bienta now. Instead, we gathered in Giles's living room to formulate a plan. Dick scribbled figures on a notepad while Sarah, Blake, and I brainstormed. For the first time, Giles revealed to all of us that his insurance coverage had been cut off several months before. A lifetime's savings in the tens of thousands that he and Bienta had set aside to pay for the children's education was tapped out, too. And bills were still coming in. No wonder Giles had looked so helpless and hopeless the other day.

Our reassurances that he and Bienta were not alone seemed to buoy him. Within the hour, the phone began to ring with support—from the church, the school, clients, and friends. One particularly well-connected customer of the Garden Shoppe corralled his wealthy friends who gladly offered donations. We like to idealize small towns and the values that go with them, but I had truly never seen an outpouring like that, and I don't expect that I ever will again. I thought I knew how loved this family was, but clearly I had no idea.

It was a Monday afternoon, but nonetheless, the atmosphere at Giles's house began to feel downright festive. A Shoppe customer who heard about the brainstorming arrived with a bag of burgers and fries and handed them out to everyone. Giles ate nothing, but he beamed relief. I asked him if he recalled a lesson he gave me as we stood beside the creek one afternoon before his stroke.

"You explained how certain plants are known to propagate

by sending seeds out on the breeze or on the rushing waters," I reminded him. "Your friendships are strong, like those plants. The word has been passed, and as a result, your family's needs will be met."

A car pulled up. Conversation ceased. It was Bienta. She trudged up the ramp on heavy feet. When she walked into the living room and caught sight of us, the expression on her face grew puzzled and her body language was defensive. She sat down and shifted her eyes from face to face. While Sarah explained to her why we were all there, Bienta's face turned into a mask of surprise, her mouth in a round and startled O. She pulled her arms together and her fingers curved into a tiny double fist, as if she sought to make herself as small as possible. My heart broke for her.

I thought of all of Giles and Bienta's dreams—that they would get their Ph.D.s and get jobs at the finest universities, save lots of money and send it back to their families in Kenya. Giles had told me once that they'd planned to go back to Kenya eventually to start a farm. Now here they were, their daughter stuck on another continent, Giles's body broken by illness, both of them working multiple jobs to make ends meet and yet still their savings were exhausted. It was easy for me to imagine that Bienta had always been the responsible, dependable one. The one whom friends relied on for her wisdom, her resources, and her generosity. And here she was, sitting in her own living room, forced to accept charity. No wonder she looked like she wanted to disappear into her own skin.

I decided that I would go to Bienta later and assure her that I understood. I knew what it was like to feel that the tables had been turned on me. Yet even as I thought this, I knew that my words would be of little help. The horrible shame of illness and need was too big to be dissolved with a few gentle sentences, no matter how well meant.

18.

Snow

Dick had made a careless error, and it wasn't like him.

Could he be rude, abrupt, downright prickly? Oh yes, all of the above. But breaking a commandment was another thing altogether. And of all the sins he might have committed, adultery was the one that was certain to hit me hardest.

It had been my worst fear, ever since I was diagnosed the first time, that Dick would leave me, that he'd grow tired of my broken body. And now the proof that he'd abandoned me was staring me in the face in the form of a size 6 woman's dress. I found it zipped up with one of his suits when I was cleaning out the guest closet. I stood there staring at it, my brain struggling to comprehend how this item of women's clothing that I had certainly never bought or worn had come to nestle against Dick's suit.

I'd never mixed pills with alcohol. In fact, I didn't drink much at all. But after finding that cozy his-and-hers packing job, I made an exception.

One Xanax. One glass of red wine. Next, I called Dick at the office. "Do you have any idea what a woman's dress would be doing zipped in one of your suit bags with your suit?"

For once, my always-faithful husband had no answer. He didn't plead work obligations or blithely say he'd check it out tonight. Before I knew it, he was home. If that wasn't proof of guilt, I didn't know what was.

I heard his key in the door and slammed my hand against the kitchen counter. I used a stool to climb up and sit on the chopping block surface, where, in anger and perhaps a little drunk, I teetered more than was really safe. But in that moment, I didn't care.

"You forgot about it, didn't you?" I said to him. "Did you need company, other than me, on your trip to Florida? Was it one of those seminars where you called me and we talked about the weather for forty-five seconds?"

"Carol, I honestly don't know what you're talking about. What did you find? Can you show me?"

I marched upstairs to the guest room. He followed me. I indicated the closet and he took out the bag, unzipped it, and slung it onto the bed. His cheeks grew red and the whites of his eyes took on a rosy hue as well. The light green dress, size 6, was on top. I reached over him, pulled it out, and held it up.

"Could I ever wear this?" I said. "Maybe in the newborn nursery. Certainly not past the age of twelve."

Dick thoughtfully handled the man's suit. I could tell he was trying hard to remember something. Then he smiled in the way you do when you're so relieved you could cry. "This isn't mine," he said. "I bought it for Chad. Don't you remember? I liked it so much that I bought one for myself, too, in a larger size. That's Ashley's dress, I believe. They had a wedding to attend when they were home for Christmas. They must have forgotten it." Dick laughed with a gasp.

I took a step backward until I reached the wall, then I slowly slid down to the floor. "I'm a horrible person. I think that sums it up."

Dick tried to pull on the jacket in the suit bag. The sleeves were inches too short. The buttons didn't reach. He laughed again and I joined in at first, then my laughter turned to weeping. He took off the coat and then, to my surprise, he gently pulled me up from the floor and took me in his arms.

We were both shaking, as if we'd just escaped being run over by a speeding train. Cancer had turned our lives upside down, and we'd lost some of our faith in how the world works. Even Dick, who knew for a fact that he hadn't cheated on me, had been terrified. My illness had threatened to tear us apart—and in my worst moments, it still felt like a shadow hanging over us. Although I'd healed physically, the deeper wounds were still there, like a form of post-traumatic stress.

Finally, he held me away from him and we looked at each other.

It was almost more than I could bear. "I'm crazy, aren't I?"

Dick held me again and assured me that I wasn't. He'd been as confused as I was. Later that evening, after dinner, and when our hearts had stopped racing, Dick suggested that we go out to dinner for our anniversary the following night. He said he'd make reservations.

The next morning, Dick and I woke up to falling snow. School was canceled and I begged him to stay home from work. But being his obsessive, firstborn self, he pressed on. I watched him cleaning off his car, and wondered if he was as energetic as he seemed, or if it was only his eagerness to escape. He'd been sweet and understanding last night, but I sensed him pulling back into his shell again, turning away from the ugly truth that we'd faced together last night—that I could die and we were terrified of losing each other.

I sipped my second cup of coffee and watched from the doorway as Dick's shovel made repeated stabs around each tire to set it free. We used to love to watch the snow together.

Dick came in for a quick kiss goodbye, then left, his footprints crisply outlined in the snow. He didn't turn back. I decided to cheer myself with wrapping the presents I'd gotten him for our anniversary—a handsome leather wallet, which he really needed, and a favorite picture of the kids, which I'd enlarged and framed for his office.

Dick phoned as soon as he got to the office to tell me that

he'd made reservations at Charlee's, my favorite restaurant, for that night. Then he added, "If you're looking for something to wear, there's a green dress in my suit bag."

The warmth had returned to his voice, and I sensed a hint of the playfulness that had always made him so attractive to me. How silly I'd been since my surgeries and chemo—doubting him, when he didn't deserve to be under suspicion, not for one second.

I tried out several outfits. A low-cut black V-necked sweater looked best—it showed off my new breasts. I still wasn't entirely used to them, but I had to admit they looked good. I decided on tan wool pants and a pair of black leather boots to go with the sweater.

Later, when Dick picked me up for dinner, he said, "Well, look at you." I wondered if he realized how long it had been since he'd given me that kind of affirmation.

That evening we sat in our favorite corner booth. The glow of candlelight cast slimming shadows on our faces. The music of a string quartet and murmurings from other diners mixed in with gently clinking tableware.

Dick gave me a single, polished amber stone set in a silver necklace. I was pleased when he told me that he'd had it custom-made. He said he returned to the jeweler three times to add tweaks and adjustments to make sure it was just what he had in mind. The necklace hung down almost to the enhanced cleavage that was still new to me. I looked up quickly from the deep V of my sweater. I wasn't accustomed to such abundance. The skin of my breasts was still numb, and I could have been spilling out without noticing it. So I kept a careful check.

I wanted to say, *We're still us. Right?* But although I desperately wanted to know the answer to that question, I kept it to myself. It would only start a testy conversation and lead to an argument.

Dick wore a passive, thin-lipped smile that was hard to read. In the wash of wobbling shadows I lifted my wineglass to my lips. I thought how, many years ago, there was a time when we were less self-conscious. One of us might have asked the playful, clichéd question:

"Happy?"

Then we both would have laughed. Now laughter was no longer easy, and every word had to be measured in advance. Still, I asked Dick the clichéd question, this time from my heart. "Happy, Dick?"

He nodded to say that he was. It struck me with fresh pain that I wasn't sure of Dick anymore. I'd always felt that Dick considered me an asset. I was nice-looking and friendly, and once I'd gotten over my youthful awkwardness, he often had me join him for social occasions with important clients. I was good at softening Dick's sharp edges—and Dick had a lot of those. I always laughed when someone in town asked me if I was the Carol Wall married to Dick Wall, the lawyer. Dick had pissed off so many people over the years that my typical response to that question was, "Well, I don't know, tell me more. Was he for you, or against you?"

Dick hadn't asked me along on a client dinner in a long time. Of course for months and months I wasn't well enough to go. Now I wondered if my absence had become a habit. I'd gone from being an asset to a liability—or perhaps a cause for sympathy. I knew that Dick had told his colleagues and clients all the gory details of my illness and in my less charitable moments I accused him of making an avocation of being the cancer spouse, the long-suffering husband. It took all the strength I had to hold on to a vision of myself that was firm and solid, and not permanently shaken by cancer. And that included how I viewed myself as a wife. It shook me to the core to realize that it wasn't enough for me to be a good wife. To hold on to my husband, I would also have to be a lucky wife to have chosen a man who would stick by me, no matter what.

At home, I opened more wine and Dick unwrapped his gifts. He especially loved the picture of our children.

I leaned over his shoulder, looking at it. "This is really a handsome group, don't you think? Those are all the children I'm going to have. I'm not so sure about you, though. You may not be finished yet."

Instantly, I knew I'd made a terrible mistake.

Dick looked at me with a wounded expression. "With you, no one can win. When you found the dress, I could defend myself. But how can I take responsibility for something that may or may not ever happen? You may outlive me. All I have to do is come home late from work and you accuse me of avoiding you, or for God's sake, having an affair. You're mad at everyone.

You're pissed at the people who sent you sentimental cards when you were sick and you're pissed at those who didn't send cards at all. Are you the only perfect person in the world? Are you some kind of saint because you have cancer? This is not my fault."

I was stunned, and I felt the velocity of our emotions increasing all around me, as if I'd fallen from a cliff but hadn't hit the ground yet. "When did things start to change? Was it the first diagnosis, or the second? The surgeries, the complications, or the chemo? Something's wrong," I insisted. "I'm not crazy to feel this way."

Our argument continued up the stairs, my footsteps pounding out a jagged rhythm on each wooden step. Dick followed me, telling me that I was in fact crazy. I replied by calling him a "rotten bastard," rage erupting inside me with a force that frightened me. I yanked the sheets and blankets from our king-sized bed and piled them on the floor. I pounded the mattress with my fist. Dick snagged my wrist and held on tightly.

"Let go!" I said, but he ignored me. "Are you sorry you married me?"

"No," he said. "Are you?"

His gaze was unwavering. It was one of the first things I loved about him, back in high school when he was willing to take a stand for something that was right, even if it meant he would be unpopular. Our sadness was like a broken wafer, half of it in his hand, half in mine. We each had our portion, and our ability to bear it was a far more meaningful token of our love than any of the happy talk we'd shared in less troubled, less tested times. I started to weep, considering all the ways I loved him. I prayed he felt the same for me. I wondered how I could ever be sure.

Later, I was calm enough to realize that no one could ever be sure. And I knew that I shouldn't still need the reassurance. I had thought I was cured of that kind of uncertainty years ago—I even remembered the exact moment when I thought I'd learned my lesson once and for all. We'd been married only a few years, and we were invited to a barbecue at a neighbor's home. They seemed perfect in every way—perfect couple, perfect kids, perfect clothes. The food and table settings were like something right out of *Southern Living*. After dinner, the husband, an amateur photographer, brought out all these gorgeous pictures he'd taken of his wife in various tasteful poses. It all seemed so romantic, and I wondered to myself, *Why doesn't Dick take pictures of me? He could at least write me a poem.* Of course, about a year later, Mr. Perfect was caught writing graphic letters to his teenage assistant and his marriage was over.

So yes, I knew better than to doubt Dick. But while some people might have pointed out to us that my illness should have brought us even closer together and deepened our relationship even further, I felt like our relationship was deep enough, thank you very much. I didn't need cancer to make me love or appreciate Dick more. I already loved and appreciated him so much that it was almost more than either of us could bear.

Dick walked away from our argument, the way he always did after an emotional storm. It was for the best, I knew. I glanced in the mirror and was shocked to see how haggard I looked. My fingers sought the smoothness of the amber stone Dick had given me. Touching it, I was given the grace to know that Dick and I would soon be face-to-face again, with our apologies at the ready. I retrieved the covers from the floor and made the bed. I spotted my marble notebook on the nightstand, and, remorseful, I began to write:

Dearest Dick,

I hope you are receiving mail this evening. And even if you are not, please do give consideration to this writer who loves you quite a bit more than you may imagine. You were right. You have done nothing to cause my suffering or your own. Still, you have not yet weathered the experience of tucking yourself into bed each night and wondering if the sun will come up tomorrow for you.

This is the hell of it. Should I succumb to my disease, much will be lost. Yet until the end, I can't help but be haunted by the specter of you putting your arms around another woman— probably younger, healthier, and a little less crazy than I.

When we were arguing, it suddenly occurred to me that I'd better do whatever it takes to make myself a little less crazy. How ironic it would be if my love for you actually made my world a sort of living death. Unlike you, I must bear some of the blame. Not everyone is perfect, like you are. ☺

Rules for a happy marriage (over Time)

1. Kiss. A lot. The world can wait.

2. Clear your mind of your imaginary troubles, as the real ones need some neurons to bounce off of.

3. *As to thoughts of "other people . . ." The spouse you*
   pledged your heart to is an "other" person. Guard your
   words and actions in the sanctity of that.

With love,
Carol

I heard Dick coming back upstairs. His footsteps were measured, a sure sign that his anger had subsided, too. I tore out the page and stashed the letter under his pillow.

19.

Tomato Plants

I celebrated the first day of summer vacation by sitting on our front porch, wearing shorts and flip-flops. Rhudy accompanied Giles as he walked slowly through the yard with stilted steps. Giles had come back to work in the spring, and Rhudy was his constant companion, somehow sensing that Giles needed watching over.

Giles leaned on his cane, engrossed in his work. He seemed to be feeling stronger each day, at a pace that matched the increase in temperature and the blooming of the flowers.

Robert Maxim's new wife wandered over, pointing toward their house and seeking Giles's wisdom on a matter in her garden. I swore I heard the word "azalea," and I winced.

As Giles spoke to her, I thought I saw a kind of resignation in the way he stood, and I hoped it was just my imagination. There was more gray threading through his hair, I noticed. He and I hadn't spoken much about his health lately. He much preferred the close inspection of a blighted leaf, or a consultation on a slug that was causing damage, to a conversation that caused him to dwell on how sick he'd been. That only led to the question that plagued my thoughts but that I hadn't dared to ask. It had now been almost two years since his stroke—would Giles ever regain what he'd lost?

Later that week, I agreed to pick Giles up from his routine doctor appointment. Returning home along the quicker back route I'd at last discovered, I was surprised when Giles abruptly called out, "Mrs. Wall, we must stop here."

He was clearly tired, but grew more cheerful as he pointed me toward some handsome-looking produce at a roadside stand. I steered my van along the uneven shoulder of the road. My tires protested with a little squeaking sound as they rolled along the asphalt, and before I solved the problem of logistics (how to go around and help Giles out, among these knee-high weeds?), I heard a creaking. Giles had already opened his car door and pushed it wide with his cane. Then he struggled out with no help from me.

His spirits lifted even more while showing me some small tomato plants he wanted me to bring home to my yard. He reminded me how important the angle of the sun would be to whether the tomatoes thrived or not. Then he stopped himself. "In any case, you're ready to be on your own," he said.

"This will be my first attempt at growing food," I said.

"Lok also is very good at cultivating," he said. "She always has a little kitchen garden."

I didn't ask about Lok. The timing didn't feel right—I sensed that it would only make Giles sad. Instead I held up one plant, and then another. He nodded and said that I had made good choices. They were healthy, green and sturdy, with nice branches, which would soon be set with tiny, star-shaped yellow flowers.

"These are the best ones, right?" I asked again, eager to meet his approval, as if I were his horticulture student and this might be weighed in my final grade.

As the vendor counted my change, I was alarmed to hear Giles stumble on the gravel. His hand went out against the makeshift produce stand, and it trembled under his weight. His mouth drooped slightly at one corner, as I'd noticed it sometimes did when he had pushed himself too far.

"What did the doctor say?" I asked, as if I had a right to know. "Are you okay, Giles?"

"I am fine," he managed to answer.

I phoned ahead to find out if the boys were at home, and then I drove Giles there. They helped us as we struggled up the ramp and through the door. With his sons giving him support, Giles sank down onto the sofa, leaning back against the cushions with a sigh. Within minutes, he began to recover. His features looked more balanced, and he asked for some water. He even said he was hungry, which I took as a good sign.

Back home, I turned my attention to the assignment Giles had given me. In the stubborn soil of my backyard, I channeled the instructions he had demonstrated over time. I heard him telling me to space the tomato plants well, allowing for their doubling in size in twelve to fifteen days. For a stronger stem, I needed to prune soon after that. One should never prune or tie plants when the leaves are wet, he had told me. You don't want them to mildew, rot, or break.

I set my gardening gloves aside to feel the warmth of the fertile soil between my fingers. It seemed like such a small thing, and yet it was monumental to me. I was suddenly reminded of Mama teaching me to ride a bike. In the first few sessions, she held on to the back of the seat, running along behind me. Then one day, when I turned around, I was astonished to see I'd left her far behind.

I felt joyful and wistful in equal measures as I guided my tomatoes' roots into the ground. So much had happened since the day I discovered Giles's loving gift of white flowers in my yard. And today I had officially become a gardener.

The rest of summer passed all too quickly. Giles and I kept up our routine of seminars and visits to my "compound." And from my kitchen window, I admired the growth of my thriving tomatoes. They were impossibly beautiful, yielding small red globes that seemed to glow in the afternoon sun.

The day before school started, I drove across town to place

my very best tomato on Giles's kitchen windowsill. I found him sitting in his wheelchair by the front window.

"Giles, you are truly a great teacher if you can help someone like me produce such beauty out of my backyard. I never dreamed I could do this."

Giles smiled. "I have always enjoyed helping others discover the process, and I find myself learning each time I work with students."

I sat down near him. I didn't want to rush this visit. With school starting again, I might not feel so free again for a while. "I've always been curious about that picture on your bookshelf, Giles, the one of you in your white lab coat, and the students proudly holding those large cabbages. Was that taken in Kenya?"

"Yes. I was teaching at Egerton College, near Nakuru. The picture was taken on a three-acre demonstration unit we had in the horticulture department. I taught vegetable production, including field preparation, rotation, irrigation, pest control, management, and even marketing. The produce was sold at reduced prices to staff and faculty." He held up a finger as if to emphasize the point he was about to make. "I always told my students that it is necessary to go out in the field. A book is just a start, and a laboratory project pales beside examination of the thing itself."

I thought of the hundreds of students who must have heard this, marching along behind their teacher in his white coat. Giles kept his eyes fixed on the photo, and I wondered if he was pondering all the future accomplishments he'd looked forward to that day. I imagined how proud he must have felt to have already taken such a big step on his and Bienta's journey toward their ultimate goals.

On the bookshelf just behind him was a leather-bound copy of his dissertation. *Giles Owita: Doctor of Philosophy in Horticulture* was stamped in gold on the spine.

These few words captured so much of the dream Giles had prepared himself to transform into reality. His education was the one part of his plan that he could control. But he couldn't account for other people's prejudice or limitations. And he couldn't make himself well. I prayed that he didn't think he had failed. I thought of his children, and how beloved he was.

"Your life is bearing fruit, as well," Giles said, as if he were channeling my thoughts. "Whatever comes, you must continue working in your garden."

"Of course," I promised him. "Whatever comes, I will keep going. And you must promise, my friend, that you'll continue working right beside me."

Giles smiled and nodded, but he didn't reply.

20.

Seedlings

As fall grew chilly and gave way to winter, Giles and I developed a regular schedule for our seminars. I went to his house every Wednesday after school, and from time to time, and when weather allowed, he came to my yard. Our garden lessons were always mixed with discussions of more wide-ranging topics. We started with our children, especially Lok, who had just taken the photo for her visa application. Then, inevitably, our conversations veered all across the map from science to philosophy and religion.

To my great delight, Bienta joined the choir in the loft for rehearsals on Thursday nights. She was welcomed warmly as we started our second week rehearsing Advent music. She sang her notes beautifully and laughed at jokes along with everyone. But I

had sensed a distance between the two of us ever since the day
we'd become aware of her and Giles's financial hardship. And I
just couldn't seem to cross that great divide. Bienta was such a
strong woman, and intimidating in her own way. I so wanted to
talk to her about Lok, and ask about Giles's health, which seemed
so frighteningly fragile to me—he'd even taken to using his
wheelchair more often again. But I felt as if Bienta hung a "closed
for business" sign over her face whenever I came near. Conversation beyond the shallowest pleasantries was rendered impossible.

So I shared my fears with Sarah instead. One Saturday when
I was browsing at the Garden Shoppe, I pulled her aside. "Do
you think Giles is losing weight? Dick says I'm imagining things.
But I don't think I am. I'm worried he has cancer and he doesn't
want us to know."

"Cancer?" Sarah said, surprised. "What makes you think he
has cancer?"

I thought about mentioning Giles's melanoma diagnosis, but
then I stopped myself. Had I become one of those people I'd always complained about, who treat other people's illnesses like
gossip? "Well, anyone could have cancer," I said.

"I don't know, Carol. I'm inclined to agree with Dick on this
one. I don't think there's any big secret there. I just think Giles
is under a lot of stress, and recovery from a stroke is so long and
arduous. I'm sure it's terribly depressing for him not to be able
to do the things he once did so easily."

Driving home, I racked my brain for ways to cheer up Giles.

Then an idea came to me. The snake plant he and Bienta had given me suffered terribly from my total incompetence with houseplants. So I made an appointment to speak with Giles at his earliest convenience about an urgent gardening matter.

"This is my confession," I told him. "I have been equally negligent through overwatering *and* under-watering, and that's the truth."

Where lesser gardeners might have chuckled, Giles found nothing to amuse him as his eyes took in the horror of the situation. The succulent whose upright, green-and-golden glory used to please had faded to a withered stalk the color of a brown paper grocery bag.

"It must be severely pruned. That is the only answer," he decreed.

He sat a little straighter in his wheelchair. Then he grasped the sofa arm to pull his chair across the rug to save the poor plant from my deadly clutches. He seemed energized, in fact, to see the plant's neglected state. He asked me to go into the yard and bring his pruning shears inside. I zipped up my jacket and started for the back door.

He called after me, "Look under the tarps and choose a specimen you like. Bring it in to me and we will work on that, too."

Outside, I stooped to lift the garish tarps I'd disrespected so many times. Underneath, I found a sight whose quiet beauty took my breath away. In the shelter of the covered chairs and benches were a host of tiny seedlings, clearly thriving. They'd all been rescued, Giles would tell me later, from other people's curbside trash. Falling to my knees to get a better look, I saw how all this while, beneath the unattractive surface, the gears of life had been turning, nature ticking beautifully along like the mesmerizing works of an expensive watch.

Dr. Giles Owita's backyard rescue project had flourished despite illness and cold winds. Finding this felt like a Christmas morning discovery of a shiny new bike under the tree. That feeling intensified as I looked under each and every tarp throughout the yard and uncovered treasures everywhere. There were countless scores of tiny pots containing little conifers, fledgling sprigs of holly, and myriad green things rescued from obscurity and tended by the greenest thumb in Roanoke.

"Mrs. Wall? Have you found what you were looking for?" Giles called to me from his back door.

I chose a tiny conifer as my specimen, grabbed the shears, and went back inside. I helped Giles roll his wheelchair to the kitchen table, situated in a charming alcove off the living room. Then I pulled out a chair and sat beside him, feeling as I always did when I watched him work—like a lucky student basking in the reflected brilliance of a gifted professor.

Hideous debris fell away from the ailing snake plant as Giles performed his regimen of snips and clips, his movements all but automatic. "This will be fine," he said. "Please take it back home with you."

Then, under Giles's instruction, I added peat moss to the soil around the feathery pine tree seedling I had chosen. When I hesitated at any point, Giles couldn't restrain his hand from reaching out to help me. Once we'd finished he said, "Let me keep this one for a little while. I will let you know when it is ready."

We settled in Giles's living room again, and as always our conversation meandered, and I waxed philosophical. "You know, I was reading the other day about Einstein's theory that space and time are elastic. What does that mean to you, Giles? Do you think it could mean that we might pass this way again?"

"This is a mystery," Giles said. "What do you think?"

"Are we speaking science, or religion?"

"Einstein said that they are one." Then he looked in my direction with that old familiar twinkle in his eye. "But I can always take the matter to my Virginia Tech doctoral panel for some further answers and get back to you."

After Christmas, Giles called to say that my little orphan tree was thriving and it was time for me to take it home.

When I stopped by Giles's house to pick it up, I found myself growing emotional as he handed it to me. I thought about how it had been thrown away as trash, then rescued to a place of nurture underneath the tarps. Now it had an opportunity to become everything it had been created for—and all because Giles had seen the potential in a scrubby little seedling.

"I want to thank you, Giles," I started to say. "Because without your expertise and patience . . ." My tears welled up and I was reminded of our son Chad, and the learning disability he'd struggled with in school. I told Giles how one of Chad's teachers had breezily informed us that he would never be college material. Now he was working on his Ph.D. dissertation.

"Oh, many, many people speak too soon," Giles said. "And those who know a little less speak even sooner. Perhaps I'll help you, one day, find that prophesying teacher with her sour-milk approach to children. She cannot be very happy. More unhappy still are the little ones who look to her for nurturing."

"Yes." I blotted my eyes and held a tissue to my nose.

Then, to my surprise, Giles's eyes filled with tears as well. "Perhaps I should not be the one to criticize. I often wonder if I have been too strict with my boys, too apt to point out the bad instead of the good. But they have always been such good boys. Now I see this more clearly. Why was I so insistent about small things that didn't really matter?"

I had never heard Giles sound so unsure of himself, so regretful. I wished I could rescue him from his uncertainty the way he'd always done for me. "Oh, Giles, there isn't a parent in the world who hasn't asked that same question. I certainly have. Half the time I thought I was being too strict, and the other half of the time I thought I was being too lenient. But you have to look at your intentions, Giles. I think that's what the Good Lord does, don't you?"

"Yes, He sees and understands all of that, and more."

Moments later, the spell of our conversation was broken when Bienta and their two sons arrived home. Giles brightened, and I excused myself to leave them to their dinner. That night, after I returned home, I placed my growing pine tree on the gate-leg table in our living room. I hoped that I had brought Giles some comfort with my visit. And I prayed that he might heal and thrive like that treasure trove of seedlings hidden beneath the nondescript blue tarp in his backyard.

21.

The River

For a long while, I'd thought that Daddy's condition couldn't possibly grow worse—and yet he continued to drift further away from me. When I visited him, I searched for signs that he remembered me, but eventually I had to admit that I had become a stranger to him. Over the course of his long and cruel illness, it was as if my father had been taken from me in pieces, bit by bit.

Then one day, he was gone entirely, and not even his shell remained.

We placed him on the hillside next to Mama. Although I'd often recoiled from the overly sweet and optimistic greeting cards that had come my way after my cancer diagnosis, I cherished each sympathy card I received after Daddy died. I knew

246 · MISTER OWITA'S GUIDE TO GARDENING

how pleased he would be by every gesture. In Radford, he was often called upon to be a pallbearer if someone died without a family or friends to give a proper send-off. I pictured Daddy, free in death, to be that kind, expansive, generous, and loving man again, and that was the greatest comfort I'd had concerning him in quite a while.

A few days after Daddy's funeral, I woke up slowly. I was conscious—I wasn't dreaming—but I felt a transporting sense of peace. I blinked my eyes, reached across the mattress, and confirmed that I was alone in the bed. Everything seemed solid, real, authentic. Dick was downstairs in the kitchen, making coffee. Light fell at a familiar angle through the narrow spaces in between our bedroom blinds. I looked toward the foot of my bed, and standing there was a little boy—brighter than the sunlight, almost golden.

He was maybe eight or ten years old, not any more than that. And as real as he appeared to me, I realized that I wasn't seeing him with my eyes, but with my being.

Perhaps he was an angel. I studied him for several seconds. His hair was blond and parted on the side. He wore a pair of denim overalls that brought to mind the Depression and life on a farm. I thought of him as being barefoot, but I couldn't see his feet.

There was another person with him, taller and protective of the boy. The gender of this taller being wasn't clear to me, but that fact seemed oddly unimportant. The taller being looked out

across the room while the little boy faced me. It was this child
who had come to see me.

By the time I scrambled out of bed, they were gone.

In my next moment of clarity, I resolved that I wouldn't tell
anyone about the incident, not even Dick. He'd surely think I'd
finally, once and for all, lost my mind.

All day, I was simultaneously shaken and comforted by my
morning vision. I wondered how I could feel both ways at once.
On the one hand, something told me that the blond-haired boy
at the foot of my bed was there to comfort me. On the other, I
thought that sane people were not visited by spirits from the
great beyond.

That afternoon, on my regular visit to Giles, I felt jumpy and
anxious. Finally, and despite my promise to myself, I decided to
confess my secret to Giles.

"Giles, do you believe the dead can visit us?"

"What Kenyans call the 'Earth Above' is always reaching
down to us," he said. He sat in his wheelchair opposite the picture window, and his voice was casual, as if he were talking about
a visit from a neighbor. "Our ancestors, who live below and furnish our foundation, bring us dreams. Those who have flown are
with us every day. This is a part of life. We accept such things as
natural and normal."

"Waking up this morning, I saw someone beside my bed.

And I can't really explain why or how I know this, but I'm pretty sure that little boy was my father."

"Okay."

"Daddy grew up on a farm and I have pictures of him wearing denim overalls, just like that little boy wore." I produced a faded photo from my purse and showed it to Giles.

He studied it, his eyes reflecting a keen appreciation of the situation.

"Now, listen, Giles. I usually hate when people tell me things like this. It always sounds made-up, like wishful thinking. At first, I promised myself I wouldn't tell a single soul, but then I thought of you. Could I be going crazy?"

He laughed. "You are not crazy. Quite the opposite. You are one of the least crazy people I know. I am glad to hear of this. Your father chose to come to you. It shows the closeness and respect you have with him, on either side of the river."

Once again I began to cry in front of Giles, and I noticed his eyes were full of emotion as well. Then tires on the driveway pierced the moment. Bienta was home.

As she entered through the kitchen door, I slipped the photo of Daddy into my purse.

"How are you, Mrs. Wall?" Bienta said.

"We're doing fine. And thank you for your card of sympathy."

"Of course," she sighed. "So many things have happened, haven't they?"

"We've all had some difficult times these past few years."

"Mrs. Wall, it has been so long since we have had time to speak," Bienta said. "I wonder if you might be free for lunch on Saturday?"

I tried to keep from showing my utter surprise. "Yes," I said. "Of course. I'd love to." I hoped my smile came across as friendly and laid-back, and not shocked and deeply curious. I couldn't help feeling that there was something Bienta had been keeping from me—something she wanted to tell me. I mentally ticked down a list of what it might be—something about Giles, medical bills, the boys' tuition. Possibly something to do with her relationship with Giles. I'd often sensed they were at odds, and if so I could certainly understand. I knew from personal experience how tough on a marriage it is when one spouse is sick and the other is well.

I scanned Bienta's face for clues. Her expression was pleasant and reserved as always, and once again she'd hung the "closed for business" sign. I wasn't going to get any more out of her until she was good and ready.

Bienta and I met at a café in town. We made small talk and placed our orders, which turned out to be exactly the same. I was determined to let Bienta bring up her mysterious subject, and not to ask any direct questions. So instead we chatted about our children.

The subject of sibling rivalry came up, and she shared the

Kenyan wisdom that when two children want a parent's attention, you always tend to the older one first. "That one knows you better and would be more hurt by having to wait," she explained.

"Really? That's fascinating," I said. "We generally do the opposite. *You're older. You can wait.* That's our philosophy. But what you say makes perfect sense. Where was such wisdom when my kids were growing up?"

We laughed a bit over that, and I was happy to see that Bienta seemed a bit more relaxed today. Then she sighed, and sadness settled over her features. "I'm afraid my daughter feels she's been forgotten."

"I'm sure she knows that isn't true, and yet I'd worry, just as you do."

Bienta pressed her lips together, as if to seal in her emotions. She nodded.

"We mothers bear the blame for many things," I said.

She rested one fist on the table. "Yes. I feel foolish for relying on the workings of a vast machine to bring her to me. Not everyone is honest, Mrs. Wall. In fact, the well-placed person can be bribed—with chaos and delays resulting. Do you see?"

"I do. And I'm embarrassed to admit that had never even occurred to me. I'm so naïve, and I haven't really traveled much."

"The world is wide," she said. "And with Giles's situation, we are simply here, and cannot go to her . . . not even for a visit. Still, there's progress, lately. I am almost sure of it, and ask the saints to help us."

"I wish I could do something to help somehow. Remember how you helped with my head wrap at a time when I was feeling so low? That was such a loving thing to do, and I will always be grateful."

She nodded acknowledgment. Her expression was pained. "Things are more complicated than you can ever guess, Mrs. Wall."

"I'm here to either listen, help, or back off. I won't be chasing you down to find out more or passing on gossip to others."

"Of course not," she said. "I think of you as one of my truest friends."

Now it was my turn to feel emotional. One of her truest friends? I had always wanted that to be true, but I felt so inadequate to the task.

We settled into silence again, and despite my better intentions I rushed to fill the void. "How do you think Giles is doing?"

"Why do you ask?"

But as open as she was before, Bienta had now shut down on me again, her face a closed mask. "I ask because I care." My voice betrayed more impatience than I meant to show, and I sensed Bienta receding even more. What had started as a pleasant ladies' lunch unraveled before my eyes.

When our waitress delivered the check, Bienta and I reached for it at the same time.

"I invited you," Bienta said.

Not wanting to insult Bienta further, I drew back my hand

and managed to topple over her water glass. The puddle spread across the table and then rushed off into Bienta's lap, drenching her light blue skirt.

Bienta studied the situation in horror for an instant, and then jumped up with a tiny cry of anguish, shoving her chair backward. The scraping of its legs on the floor created a high-pitched echo. Other diners turned to gawk. I grabbed an extra napkin from the table next to us and flailed madly at the mess I'd caused.

When the restaurant manager came over to offer Bienta a clean towel, instead of accepting it she wove her way through the tables toward the exit, as if fleeing the scene of a crime. I paid our bill and then rushed out to find her.

Outside, Bienta leaned against a lamppost, sobbing, a lacy handkerchief covering her face.

"I'm so, so sorry," I said. "I'd so hoped to have a nice lunch with you and then I went and threw cold water all over it."

She nodded. "It's not your fault. And it's not the water that upset me."

"What aren't you telling me, Bienta? I truly just want to be your friend. I hope you don't mind that I visit Giles so often. He's your husband, and I have my own, if that's the problem. Look, I don't have to stop by every week. We'll put a space between us, if you'd like."

Almost instantly, her crying ceased. She looked surprised, and then regretful. "Oh, no," she answered in alarm, her earnest eyes on me. "In fact, we do appreciate, and need . . ." Her voice trailed off. "You are already a better friend to me than you know.

When you are helping my husband, you are helping our household. Someday we will explore the topic more."

Bienta reached out and put her hand on my forearm. I looked at her and said, "Well, *wabironenore*. Giles taught me that."

She squeezed my arm. "Yes, we will see each other later."

I watched as she walked uphill to where she was parked. Once again I felt shortchanged, and I wondered if Bienta would ever confide in me. I so wanted to be deserving of her trust.

My steps were slow as I found my own van. "One of these days," I said to myself, "I will know more."

22.

An Awkward Path

Days later I arrived home from school to a stunning voice mail.

Listening to the message, I briefly doubted my ears. In an irrational moment of optimism I thought, *There must have been some sort of mix-up. That awful news wasn't intended for me.*

Yet I knew that it was. The female caller, an assistant in my Handsome Oncologist's office, started with words I have already, in my journey as a cancer patient, come to dread:

"This message is for Carol Wall . . ."

I listened again. Disbelief was all I felt.

No. Impossible. Not me.

Not me, again.

I put the phone down gingerly, as if my every action posed

hidden dangers and bombs lay all around me. It had been three years since chemo ended, and my most recent routine checkup had been good. My Handsome Oncologist and I discussed a host of unrelated topics, in our usual, friendly way. He assured me that everything looked fine. The only thing left to check were my tumor markers, and I chatted with the nurse the way I always did while she drew the blood. I wasn't worried. My tumor markers had never varied in the slightest.

Until now. The new results were in, and the numbers were creeping up.

The room seemed to tilt. I called Dick at the office. He didn't answer, and I told myself that this wasn't the kind of news I should leave him in a message.

I was seized with an urge to run away, as if I could outpace my own cancer markers. There was only one person I could imagine talking to right now, and I yearned for his calming presence. Giles. I needed to see Giles.

I was terrified and angry as I drove along the back roads to his house. I thought how it would not be too much of a tragedy if, at the intersection, I forgot to brake and let a truck make simple work of me. It was a sin, I was pretty certain, to think this way. Yet trying to be virtuous had gotten me nowhere, so I gave in to bitterness.

It was a gray and blustery spring day, close to the dinner hour. The light was just fading when I arrived, and I saw Giles taking halting steps toward his garden shed, cane in hand.

The one thing I had prayed for in the past few minutes was

now close at hand. And then I heard it, the melodic voice of Giles addressing me, the sound of it a blessing on the breeze.

"Eh! Mrs. Wall!" he called to me.

We walked toward each other, meeting at his fence. His living workshop stretched out behind him, all the little plastic pots beneath the tarp. I hadn't noticed how high the magnolia had grown. I remembered how sad and frail it looked to me when I first saw it.

I struggled to keep my voice calm. "I'm glad you're here, because I thought you ought to know . . ."

He turned his head and narrowed his eyes. As always, he looked toward me but not at me. "What is wrong?"

"I don't know how to say it. I . . . well, that is, judging from some tests I had the other day, and unexpectedly, to say the least, considering results supposedly obtained . . ."

"You've learned . . . ?"

"My breast cancer markers are rising, Giles. It might mean nothing . . . or it might mean . . . anything and everything." My voice broke. "The worst. You know?"

With his cane, it took him three tries to flip the latch on the gate. "Come in," he said, "and tell me more."

"I'm going to have to have some scans. Repeated scans, the doctor said when I returned the call." I looked up at the wispy clouds that alternately raced and idled as they shifted their gears across the sky. This is exactly what I had feared all of the years since Mama and Daddy told me about the radiation treatments I'd received as a baby—this feeling that I could never, ever get free, and that it would just keep coming back. I had never told Giles about the radiation. Dick was the only other person who knew. I wasn't sure who I was protecting more by keeping this from everyone else—my own privacy or my parents' feelings. But both of my parents were dead now. "For years, Giles, my parents kept a terrible secret from me. And I've learned that secrets can be damaging to the soul."

I told Giles everything then—how I'd cried all the time as a baby, and how desperate Mama and Daddy were.

Giles looked alarmed. He turned his head as if listening for incoming artillery.

"I was only five months old. We lived in Radford then. They took me to the big city of Roanoke for three full treatments of radiation to my thymus gland."

Giles shook his head. "Radiation exposure. That is very, very bad. Especially for a baby."

"I know. Mama and Daddy meant well. We all know that now. They already had one baby with serious health problems, so I guess this doctor wanted to help them or something. In any case, it was a gross overreaction. I feel sorry for them now, and I've tried so hard to understand what they were going through, but I'm also angry. I had a small benign tumor removed from my neck when I was twelve, and another when I was seventeen. But my parents never told me why, not until Dick and I were already married. And ever since then, I've felt like my own body was booby-trapped, and it was my job to examine every inch of its terrain, like it was enemy territory. Now my worst fears are coming true."

Giles nodded, taking in everything I said, rolling my words around in his head the way he always did.

"You know, I'd like for everyone to just go away," I said. "I really would. The prodders and the pokers. The experts trained to peer and stick and cut. The ones who read charts and type up notes. The ones who train their X-rays on the innocent and hold their glowing film up to the light before surprising you with secrets you've been keeping from yourself. I feel so alone, Giles. Like I've been marked—singled out."

"I understand," Giles said. "Whenever we must carry a health legacy from the past, it can be too much to bear."

A cold wind swept across the yard just then. Instinctively, we turned to face the mountains, but in pivoting, Giles became unsteady on his feet.

"Oh, Lord," he said. His cane slipped from his grip. I tried to grasp it as it fell, but missed. The grass received it, shuddering, His cotton shirt blew up against his chest. I saw how thin he had become.

"I've upset you. That was selfish. I'm so sorry, Giles."

One of Giles's neighbors checking mail across the street called out to ask if we needed any help. She lingered at her mailbox, pretending to inspect the hinge, when all the while I sensed that she was just one of those people who had radar for gossip of any kind. I told her, no. We were fine. Giles and I dropped our voices to a whisper.

"This morning, we received some news as well," Giles said, while I retrieved his cane. "Lok's visa is going to come through.

We've known this was a possibility for quite some time, but now it is confirmed. It is a matter of days."

"Oh, Giles! That's wonderful. We'll have a celebration when she gets here." I stepped closer to him, hoping to convey how excited I felt about Lok's arrival.

If only I had known about the good news, I would have waited to share my burden with him. But his troubled expression persisted. I expected him to be overjoyed, but instead he looked sadder than I'd ever seen him.

"There is something which I have not told you," he said. "It is regarding my condition." He paused. "It is something that makes Lok's arrival a matter of the greatest urgency. I have wanted, many times, to tell you . . . of the underlying reason for this stroke and my decline . . . but we were always working in the garden and the moment never came."

His eyes shone in their earnest way, and I waited patiently for him to continue. A plane was descending toward the airport, a view that always reminded me of Lok. I watched its birdlike profile sweep along, decelerating, stretching out its belly for the landing. Giles waited until the neighbor disappeared into her house before he spoke again.

"I will not get better," he said.

"Of course you will. My mother was much older and her stroke was worse."

"No. It is not the stroke. Please listen for a moment."

He turned his face away from me. The clothesline bobbed up and down, reminding me of the jump ropes we used as children.

I noticed that Giles had finally made a key for the garden shed, but he'd left it hanging on a nail right next to the lock.

"I am HIV-positive," he said at last. "It has been this way for many years. I have lived a long time since my diagnosis, but the doctors do not believe I have much more time left."

I couldn't help myself. I gasped. Then just as quickly I thought that I must have misunderstood him. Speechless, I handed him his cane and then led him to the fence so he could grasp it for support.

"I was diagnosed in Blacksburg, fourteen years ago. My shame was profound, and the counselors made no attempt to alleviate our pain. At the time, they told me I had three more years to live. The boys were small, and they urged us to make a will, as if it was a given that Bienta would be taken, too."

"Oh, Giles, I'm so sorry." Words failed me. I thought of this awful secret that Giles and Bienta had kept tucked inside them for so long. I remembered all the times that Bienta had been on the verge of telling me something, how vulnerable she must have felt, how sick with worry and fear.

"It doesn't matter how they treated me, back then," Giles said. "You recall the hysteria in those years. Such a diagnosis was perceived as a death sentence. There was no effective treatment available. There was one person in our apartment complex whom we suspected may have intercepted a message from the doctor's office. We watched this person every day. Did he know? If so, what might he do? Call the health department? Spread the word on campus? We lived in constant dread of discovery."

I raised my hands to my face. "Oh, God, I can't believe what you have been through."

"The stigma has been almost as bad as the disease itself. Bienta has had to live with that, and worried that word would spread and the children would be treated as lepers. We told no one at Virginia Tech. And no one here in Roanoke knows, except for you, Mrs. Wall. One cannot trust many people in this life of ours."

My heart broke for Bienta. How often I'd misunderstood her diffidence. I'd thought her reserved and distant, difficult to know.

"Bienta has proved strong," Giles said, "and has been spared. Her tests are negative for the disease. The children, too."

"I'm glad for that, but I am so sorry, Giles, that you have had to keep this awful secret."

"Had Bienta sent me back to Kenya," he said, "away from the treatment available here, I would quickly have died. This is why I could never go to Lok. Who knows what obstacles might be encountered when traveling outside the country? I have not felt free to tell Lok. It would only have added to her pain. But recent blood counts have introduced a sense of urgency. She must come to me, to say goodbye. The end could quickly come."

I had no idea what to say, and I wanted only to reach out to Giles physically, to show him that I was here with him and that he was right to tell me. But I knew it would have been considered rude in his culture, and would only have embarrassed him. Instead, I grasped the fence and struggled to keep my balance.

I looked up and discovered that Giles was staring at me. He looked directly into my eyes, something he had never done before. The sky didn't fall, and he didn't turn away. I had always known that his eyes were the same deep, dark brown as mine. I wondered if he knew it, too, before this moment.

We held our gaze, and I made sure that he was the first to look away. I wanted him to know that I would never reject him. I would never turn away.

He did not tell me how he contracted the disease, and I didn't ask—nor would I ever. Each of us was too respectful of the other to cross the careful boundaries we'd kept all through the years, a man and a woman happily married to others but finding unique joy in our friendship.

"What can I do to help?" I said.

His answer came without delay. "The minute we are notified that Lok is on her way, you must assist me. You must take me out to meet her. I will be there, even at the airport, because in every moment, there exists a lifetime. Will you do this, Mrs. Wall?"

"I will."

I took my place beside Bienta in an empty corner of the bleachers. The Owita boys were playing soccer, and I had offered to keep her company.

After Giles told me his secret, I decided to abandon my random fears about the numbers someone had divined in the oncology lab. Instead, I focused on the joy of anticipating Lok's arrival.

If Bienta and Giles could celebrate at a time like this, then certainly I could as well. Meanwhile, I hoped our friendship would strengthen all of us.

Bienta's relief that Giles had confided in me was palpable, as if a thick layer of guilt and shame had been chipped away from her, and she could finally breathe and move freely.

She said that for a long time she had pleaded with Giles to tell me, and that she had so often wanted to tell me herself. But she felt both too respectful of Giles's privacy, and also too ashamed. "At first, we thought he had malaria. Early symptoms may be similar. But we were wrong. And when this came to light . . ." Her soft voice broke. "His diagnosis came when antiviral drugs were in their infancy and a pronouncement of AIDS amounted to a death sentence. Remember the quilts mothers used to sew in memory of their loved ones who were carried off by AIDS? At that stage in the research, such a loving gesture was all that could be offered. Even family members stood in danger of becoming outcasts should the secret be disclosed. We lived in fear, Mrs. Wall. We felt like criminals. Life was a nightmare."

"Yes, I do remember how it was back then," I said. "We were all so stupid, as if being in the same room with someone, or shaking their hand, might expose us. And the judgments people made. The blame. The rest of us are the ones who should be ashamed, not you."

"The stigma at that time was great," she said. "As I sent our older son to the bus each day for kindergarten, I would quickly check the door of our apartment to see if anyone had defaced it with AIDS graffiti or splashed blood across its surface."

"Oh, my God. Did people actually do that? That's terrible."

"Exactly. So, Mrs. Wall, this is how we lived."

I saw the water racing toward her on our tabletop at lunch that day. I was just beginning to understand the horror she had faced all this time—the suffocating grief, fearing for her own health, imagining how a beloved child who left lightheartedly in the morning might return the same day under the weight of accusation, a leper-by-proxy and an exile.

Bienta said, "So many times I felt I should tell you, but I always lost my nerve. Many times, I have tried, knowing it was wrong to keep this from you."

I shook my head in sympathy. "It wasn't wrong to keep it from me. I had no right to know. But now that I do know, I can help more." Bienta's degree of isolation was difficult to comprehend. If only I had been more attentive. More inclined to look beneath the surface. "I'm so sorry, Bienta. I knew there was something wrong, but I was so caught up in my own problems. I should have asked more questions instead of making assumptions. I even thought at one point that you didn't like me, and that you resented my help. Meanwhile, you were going through such torture, and all alone. I hope you can forgive me."

"You are our friend," Bienta said, her voice warm with compassion. "You have been steady on an awkward path. And as my husband says, we're going to need you more than ever, going forward."

23.

The Lilies of the Field

Giles poked his cane along the ramp into his house. The neighborhood was decorated for Halloween, with ghostly flags and black-and-purple wreaths and tiny blinking orange lights in windows.

Giles's friend Blake helped him in as I held the door. Bienta carried Giles's suitcase in. Giles was home from a brief stay in the hospital, where he'd agreed to participate in a study providing experimental treatments to patients suffering from HIV-AIDS. Bienta was happy for Giles to participate. "It is this type of research that may lead to better treatment," she said. That thought seemed to buoy Giles as well. We'd both noticed how his mood had seemed to brighten with a renewed sense of purpose when the volunteer came to take him to the hospital.

The circle of trust had expanded, if only slightly. I'd been given permission to tell Dick, and Giles and Bienta had told Blake and Sarah as well. Among us, we tried to lighten their load. While Bienta raced off to her second job, Blake headed out to do their shopping, and I stayed behind with Giles. I had brought a small stack of papers to grade, and felt guilty once again that I complained about my burdens when other people bore up under such awful things, and without a whimper.

Giles and I settled into the living room and took turns exchanging optimistic words about the other's future.

"Your scan last week was normal," Giles reminded me.

"But I have to have another one in six weeks," I said. "My doctor says that everything looks fine, but the scans must continue as long as the markers are increasing. Let's face it. Worry never ends. At least it seems that way for us."

"Yes, we are doomed to constant vigilance," he said.

"We have our own club," I said. "The downside is that it's a club no one wants to join. The upside is that we can talk about anything we want to, and no one can accuse us of being morbid. And it's oddly liberating. No one chides us about our weight or our triglycerides. There's no one to impress, and nothing else to be lost."

"It's very true," Giles said. He picked up a sky-blue leather book from his TV tray. I had seen it before, when Giles was hospitalized for his stroke. It was a small New Testament, in Luo, with a simple gold cross stamped on the front. He handed it to me and I opened it. Paging through, I marveled that the letters grouped so strangely to my eye translated more or less exactly into the words of faith so familiar to my heart.

"Giles, I feel like I may be failing this part of our seminars. Some days I have a difficult time maintaining my optimism. I tell myself not to, that it's self-defeating and pointless, but still sometimes I can't keep myself from standing in front of the mirror, just to check one more time. It's like I'm looking for trouble." I flipped through the pages some more. "Let's see if I can find the part about the lilies of the field. I'm in sore need of some inspiration."

"Let me read it to you," he said. "I find it restores my spirits." He read the first few verses in his mother tongue, and then, with equal ease, he finished the passage in the English language of the Kenyan schools where he easily excelled as a child. "'Therefore take no thought, saying, "What shall we eat?" or, "What shall we drink?" or, "Wherewithal shall we be clothed?" For after all these things do the Gentiles seek, for your heavenly Father knows that you have need of all these things.'"

"That has been my problem," I said. "I worry too much about things I cannot control."

"Father Matthews came to see me yesterday," Giles said. "He brought Communion. I spoke my heart to him. He's such a good man. Very, very good."

"He did the same for me when I was in the hospital," I said.

"I spoke to him about how I have struggled with regret. I find myself wishing I could live to see my grandchildren. But such is not my lot." His voice was simple and steady, though his words were filled with sadness. "I have been thinking about how it's all gone by so quickly, and I was so impatient as a father. When my youngest was ten or eleven years old, he had a terrible fear of spiders. He'd wake up in the night screaming with terror. I used to scold him for being frightened of something so silly. Now I realize what a sensitive person he is, and how I wouldn't wish him to be any other way."

"Giles, you mustn't torture yourself with the times you made mistakes. We all have those. Please don't forget all the wonderful things you did, too. Think of all the hours and hours you spent at soccer practice and swim meets."

He smiled, even laughed a little. "I used to love the swim meets. I loved watching them cut through the water. I'd sit right up close to the edge of the pool with my timer. The water would splash over my feet and legs, but I didn't care. So long as my boys were happy with their performance, that was what mattered to me."

"And that's what matters to them, too. They love you, Giles, the same way I know that my children love me. We all make mistakes. We just have to pray that the ones we made with our children were small ones. Only time will tell."

I mentioned an old Methodist hymn, "My Times Are in Thy Hands." I sang a few of the verses.

My times are in Thy hand; My God, I wish them there;
My life, my friends, my soul I leave entirely to Thy care.

My times are in Thy hand; Whatever they may be;
Pleasing or painful, dark or bright, As best may seem to Thee.

My times are in Thy hand, I'll always trust in Thee;
And, after death, at Thy right hand I shall forever be.

I glanced around Giles's living room at the many books on his shelves. I wished they held the answer to my questions about time and death and what came after. But I would have to accept the uncertainty.

The silence that descended around Giles and me was comfortable, as if our priest had called for prayer. I cherished the moment and it occurred to me that friendship itself could be a kind of church.

"I have thought of you as my best professor," I told Giles at last.

"And you have been my most promising student," he replied. Our matching brown eyes burned with tears.

24.

Rolling Waters

A few days later, Giles made his final visit to our yard. We both were aware of this, but it remained unspoken. His elder son came with him and we watched as Naam planted a shrub under the ancient dogwood by the creek. Giles told me it would bloom in the spring, and he surveyed the bank as if to commit it to memory.

Joining him by the fence, I saw he was weary, though I could still sense the fundamental luminosity that made him so different from anyone else I'd ever known. He paused for a moment as we watched the churning waters of the creek that swept past us, swollen from a recent spell of autumn rain.

Giles said, "Can you picture the cattle that must have grazed here in those long-ago days when this was a working farm?

Flowing water is essential. And many on the planet go without it." He walked around the fence, his labored steps unsteady on the creek bank. I imagined him falling in, and in this vision, I'm dismayed to watch him being swept downstream before my grasping hands can catch him. With careful steps, I joined him on the bank. It seemed there was something on his mind, and now he spoke of it, his eyes focused on the rolling water.

"Do not be too hard on your parents, Carol. The harm they brought into your life was unintentional. Many of us would like the chance to go back in Time, but such things are not possible here. Not even Einstein could arrange for such a thing."

I thanked him. It was the first and only time he'd ever called me by my given name.

The long-awaited good news from Nairobi came at last. Meanwhile, though only a few days had passed since his visit to my yard, Giles had entered into an irreversible decline. He clung to life, knowing that Lok was on her way. Bienta called to ask if I would drive her to the Raleigh airport to pick up Lok.

When I arrived at their home, Giles greeted me from his seat in the wheelchair by the picture window in the living room. Bienta had been detained, he said, but would be arriving momentarily.

"Why don't you go back and lie down?" I said. "I'll help you. Then you'll be stronger for Lok's arrival."

He shook his head. "If I lie down, I will not get up again."

A single tear spilled onto his cheek. I knew he was frightened of dying before Lok made it home. I gave him a tissue so he could wipe his tears.

For a moment, I had a horrifying flash of anxiety—I wondered if it might be possible to catch his disease from a tear-stained tissue. Just as quickly I knew it was ignorant and idiotic—shameful. That is what fear of illness does to people—to me. It takes away our powers of logic and compassion and separates us from each other. The specter of death and decay brings an impulse to turn away. I of all people should have known better. I still had so much to learn.

Some moments passed. Giles wiped his tears away and I wiped mine. I recalled the words Giles offered me that evening of my cancer diagnosis when I had impulsively confessed my illness to him in the Foodland parking lot. "You are not responsible for this disease," he told me that night. Now I tried to find the right words to comfort him.

"You are not alone, Giles," I said. "And there is no point in blaming yourself, or feeling ashamed. Bad things happen to the good. There are people who drown on summer vacations. There are even babies born with cancer. Many people had the right-of-way. Yet they lie smiling sadly in their coffins."

Giles nodded. "Let's not forget innocent victims of war, famine, and earthquakes. And though many advances have been made toward treatments of HIV-AIDS, the stigma has lingered for more than twenty years."

"There's nothing fair about it," I said. "And no disease on earth is reserved for guilty people."

He bowed his head, receiving this absolution. Receiving it myself, I did the same.

When Bienta and I first saw Lok, she was in the luggage area poised by a pay phone. As we descended the escalator, it seemed she was rising toward us like an earthly angel entering our lives. After all these years of dreaming about this moment, she had come to symbolize a sort of guardian angel to me—or a blessing.

She had Bienta's prominent cheekbones, and her father's brilliant smile flashed back in response to my own. She was just over five feet tall, but her hair, swept up into a bun and intricately braided, made her seem a bit taller. She wore jeans and a white linen shirt, and had slung a denim jacket over her shoulder. It slid off as she rushed toward her mother, and I picked it up. Bienta folded Lok into her arms and they spoke in either Swahili or Luo. They were so excited that it was hard to tell which.

On the drive home, a cold November rain began to fall. In the backseat, Lok fell asleep on a pillow. Bienta sat in the passenger seat and acted as navigator. From time to time she turned to watch the shadows shift across her daughter's face.

Fog descended and road signs were obscured along the winding route. Bienta had assured me that she knew the way, and had traveled these roads many times while driving the boys to their soccer games. But I wasn't at all sure where we were. I glanced at the gas gauge and noticed that it was near empty. I should have filled up before.

Bienta seemed uneasy also. Finally, she turned to me and said, "Mrs. Wall, I'm afraid I have misdirected us."

I should have remained calm. I knew well enough that panicking when you are lost only makes the situation worse. But I thought about Giles, and his terror of dying before he could see Lok. I couldn't bear the thought of arriving at their home only to find out that we were too late. My heart raced and I thought I might cry.

Then I thought of one of Daddy's favorite war pictures that he kept in his room. In it, he is driving a jeep and smiling wide for the camera. I remembered the story of how, after the war, he visited the parents of a young soldier who had died from his battle injuries while being transported in the back of Daddy's jeep. Daddy didn't know the parents and would never see them again, but he made the long drive to Belvedere, Maryland, he said, because he wanted to let them know that their only child had not died alone. He had died a hero's death, and slipped peacefully away, covered by a blanket in the back of Daddy's jeep.

It was comforting now to think of Daddy, a leader and protector, friend to those in trouble. I felt him within me, and heard his voice in my head, telling me that it was going to be all right, that we'd find our way home.

And we did. We arrived at the Owitas' house just after midnight. The wheelchair was empty, but light glowed from Giles's bedroom. The boys greeted their sister, and they all hurried back to see Giles. I heard his cry of delight at the sight of his beloved Lok. In English, he told her that he would bring her roses in summer. As she answered in another language, I prayed for it to be true, and that all of our tears would be wiped away one day.

The next day, Bienta called to say that Giles had asked for me. The time for parting was near.

When I arrived, Giles was lapsing in and out of delirium, often confusing names—all except for one, Lok. He held her by him, insisting she must remain at his side.

At last, I knew it was time to speak the words of my heart, the ones I'd been dreading having to say out loud. "I will help take care of your family, Giles. Because you would do the same for me."

His lids fluttered. There was a fleeting moment when I saw them open, and it seemed to me that he used all his energy to look directly at me one more time. He didn't say anything. But he looked into my eyes, and the final agreement of our friendship was sealed. It rested on the purest, most beautiful and logical of foundations.

In the bedroom doorway going out, I paused for one last

look. His hands lay atop the crumpled sheets. Their veins suggested the powerful confluence of many tiny rivers.

"Wabironenore," I whispered. "Do you remember the day you taught me the Luo way to say 'farewell'?"

We would see each other later; it was true. He couldn't respond, and yet I heard him promise.

25.

All the Things He Loved

A POEM FOR MY FRIEND GILES:
There's a way of passing through that's difficult
And one that's easy.
A breath that you take and you hold,
And after that, a burning brightly.
The love that you hold for your fellow man
Can never be extinguished.
Lie down by the stream
And may Paradise be.

It was a bright November morning. The sky was periwinkle streaked with dazzlingly white clouds. Sarah hurried down the sidewalk toward me, carrying a narrow box.

I met her in my driveway, wearing my best black dress, smoothing my hair into shape and twisting my key in the back of the van to let the hatch up.

"Let me have a peek," I whispered.

Sarah's eyes were tearful, but she smiled. "At first, I could find nothing. And then, as I walked along Giles's yard, just like we hoped, I felt that he was directing me. Telling me, 'Keep looking! Don't give up! It's over here, and all you have to do is find it!'"

She pulled the lid up, and I gasped. There in the box was the spray for Giles's casket, taken from all the things he loved, the place he loved, the work he was put on earth to do. Sarah's tears began to flow.

"I just didn't think I could do it," she managed to say.

I fingered the glossy magnolia leaves from the tree by the garden shed, the narrow strips of green foliage from the yellow-bearded irises Giles loved, sprigs of holly from his backyard workshop, purple beautyberry taken from beneath the picture window, branches of juniper from beside the little summer garden, and sprigs of fragrant rosemary from that certain spot where the handicapped ramp started upward from the sidewalk toward the front door. That's where a visitor would always hear Giles calling, "Eh! *Amosi!* Please come in!"

I took the box from Sarah and placed it carefully in the van. We embraced as neighbors passing by in cars looked on in sympathy, and now I was weeping, too. Several of these neighbors would attend the Mass, along with so many others who had come to know Giles and were grateful for the blessing of his fruitful life.

Dick dropped me off at the back entrance to the church and went around to park. I heard the choir rehearsing the Crimond (The Lord's My Shepherd) for after Communion, and I knew the joyful strains of "All Things Bright and Beautiful" would soon be rehearsed, as well.

I carried the arrangement into the chapel, where Bienta and the children waited. They watched me as I held Sarah's arrangement, Giles's masterpiece, over the polished wood of the closed casket. I carefully lowered it into place.

My gaze focused briefly on the brilliant orange rose hips taken from bushes that only weeks before swayed majestically in the breeze, heavy with roses awaiting a traveler's arrival. This gave way to a view of the lovely traveler herself. Lok stood on the other side of the narrow coffin. Her braided hair was pulled elegantly up. She looked regal, dignified. Just like her parents. I didn't know Lok at all, not really, but she looked back at me with lively eyes that were so familiar. Tears streamed down her face, and I wanted to go to her. Then Bienta and the boys moved closer in, and I held back. As they formed a circle, Bienta's gracious arms reached out to include me.

I counted forward in time. How many weeks would pass before summer came again? And when did the roses bloom last year? I would find the answers in the notes I'd made in my marble notebook, hopefully. Or maybe I'd simply remember the lessons conveyed by a man who taught me, at last, to love flowers. I placed my hand on the polished wood that held the body of my friend. Its surface felt so very smooth, and there was comfort, just in that. I took my loving leave of Giles and climbed the stairs to join the choir.

Epilogue

I sat by the window in my study, looking out. Summer had arrived in my yard again, but without Giles, it didn't feel the same.

The shrub that Naam planted that final day by the creek had at last sported its blossoms of bright red and yellow. As I noticed this, the hummingbird I'd been seeing for several days dipped through the yard yet again, hovering above Giles's bush and drawing nectar from the blooms.

At noon, I joined Bienta for lunch. We'd become regulars, and the hostess showed us to our favorite table. I told Bienta how the shrub had been attracting a lovely hummingbird that visited often.

She held her spoon of tomato soup aloft. "A hummingbird is visiting your yard?"

"That's right. Down on the bank. I showed you the shrub we planted. Remember?"

She sank back in her chair. I asked what was wrong.

"Did you not know about the hummingbird?" she said.

"What do you mean?"

In a mesmerized tone of voice, she told me about a humming-bird who visited Giles each day at the picture window last summer, as he was sitting in his wheelchair. It seemed to come out of nowhere, and would simply hover in midair, looking at him through the glass. "The boys liked to tease their father, calling the creature his pet," she said.

"No," I said. "A hummingbird? He never mentioned it." My heart was beating rapidly.

"We have looked in vain for that hummingbird this season," she said. "It is nowhere to be found. It has not visited our yard at all this year."

I gave a tiny gasp. We stared at each other, only somewhat disbelieving—after all, we were dealing with Giles—until the waitress returned to see if everything was all right.

"We're fine," I said.

"More or less," Bienta added. She offered me a wistful smile. "We have learned a lot, haven't we, Mrs. Wall?"

"We have."

Driving home, I remembered reading something about hum-mingbirds. It was lovely, yet unsettling, and I couldn't recall the specifics. As Rhudy enthusiastically greeted me at the door, it suddenly struck me. I rushed upstairs to my dresser and pulled out the stack of get-well cards from my surgery and chemotherapy. I had bundled them with a rubber band and buried them beneath my carefully folded T-shirts. Removing the rubber band, I thumbed through the stack until I found it. It was a card with a hummingbird logo on the back. Below the logo was the notation: "Legend has it that the hummingbird is able to float free of Time."

I pressed the stack of greeting cards to my chest and closed my eyes. What other surprises waited for me around the river's bend? I went to my study, where my marble notebook occupied a special corner of the desk. Something told me that I wasn't finished writing in it yet. I looked out at the creek. I saw my face reflected in the windowpane.

Giles, tell me—what about the next scan and the next? What will my counts be? What will my future bring? I simply have to know.

No definite answer was forthcoming. The hummingbird was not in evidence either, but Giles's cane stood in a shadowy corner by my desk. I considered what might have been Giles's greatest lesson to me—his example of the gracious acceptance of the handicaps and afflictions life had brought him. He had shown me that the earth is full of hidden treasures.

I heard Giles's voice as he softly whispered, "In every moment there exists a lifetime. Every day brings something good!"

Author's Note

This memoir is based on a true story. Names of individuals—
and certain other identifying information—have been changed
to ensure privacy. In a few instances, the time line has been com-
pressed or otherwise altered slightly to serve the purposes of the
narrative. Conversations reflect my best recollections. All perti-
nent medical information concerning the principals (HIV,
stroke, and breast cancer histories) is precisely accurate, and a
matter of record.

Acknowledgments

It takes a lot of people to make something like this possible. When I think of everyone I need to thank, I'm not sure where to start.

Maybe I should thank all the agents who turned me down over the years. They made it possible for me to find Marly Rusoff, uber-agent, and the best friend and mentor any writer could have. I had the story, but Marly made this book possible. She has a great feel for storytelling and a great feel for people. She has talked me off the ledge more than once over the last three years. She is the best.

Maybe the best thing Marly did was to get me and *Mister Owita* to Amy Einhorn at Penguin. I remember my first conversation with Amy. She had only read the proposal at that time, but told me she could "see" the book. I have no doubt that was the case. She has a gift for knowing what I am thinking and telling me how I should express it. To say she is a meticulous editor is an understatement. I know much has been written about her attention to detail. Every time she touched the manuscript, she made it better. She and her assistant, Liz Stein, have had the vision and determination to make this happen. Lots of other people at Penguin have had a hand in this, of course, including Katie McKee in Publicity and Diana Van Vleck and all of the talented sales people.

I also want to thank my friend and literary consultant, Peternelle Van Arsdale, of PVA Books, who used her special gifts and keen ear to help me find the best way to tell this beautiful story. Peternelle and I have had a special connection, and I am fortunate to have her assistance.

Lots of my friends and many in our large extended family have helped me produce this work. My husband, Dick, has encouraged me in what I used to call "my pretend writing career" for many years. He insisted that I spend the time that it takes to do this and made it possible for me to devote myself to the lonely business of writing. My children, Chad, Jennie, and Phil, also have provided support and approval. Phil had an important part in the development of the book. In 2009, shortly after Giles died, I was struggling with a manuscript about my breast cancer. "Struggling" is really putting it mildly. I was afraid of exposing my feelings and I was just not in love with the story. Just when I was about to give up, Phil suggested that I bring my friend Giles into the picture. Good idea, Phil.

Chad's wife, Ashley, and Jennie's husband, Kenny, have been supporters from the beginning. I have been inspired by a large and loving family, including my precious grandchildren, Madeline, Caroline, Rachel, and David. How can I not feel lucky?

Dick is a business lawyer, and one of his best professional qualities is knowing that he does not know everything. He also realized that being married is hard enough without adding a lawyer-client relationship to the mix. Dick introduced me to entertainment lawyer Kirk Schroder, who has provided help and advice over the last few years.

This story, of course, is about my friend Giles. I know that not many people are blessed to have such a friend, and I thank God for sending Giles into my life. I also thank my friend Ellen, master gardener, for introducing me to Giles, for being a sounding board throughout the whole process, and for providing lots of background information. My good friend Anne has encouraged me every step of the way. My PEO sisters have been a great source of strength, as has my friend Gerda. Monsignor Tom Miller has provided lots of inspiration and prayer on my journeys. Special thanks also go out to Kelly Wheelbarger and my friends in the choir.

Giles's wife, Bienta, has become a special friend, and she is an important part of the story. She has supported every part of the project and I look forward to working with her in spreading the message of *Mister Owita's Guide to Gardening*.

My struggles with cancer and my medical record are well documented in this book. For some reason, I have always avoided the term "breast cancer survivor." I have now learned to embrace being a "breast cancer patient." The many of my sisters who have this disease and share this label understand that, even though there is no cure yet, we now have the possibility of living with the disease for many years. My Handsome Oncologist, Dr. Bill Fintel, has helped me understand this. At the end of the book, I say, *"Giles, tell me—what about the next scan and the next? What will my counts be? What will my future bring? I simply have to know."* As Giles taught me, I don't really have to know. No one knows. But, Dr. Fintel and I have a plan. He is fifty-seven and plans to work until he is seventy. I plan to be at the retirement party.

My wonderful internist, Dr. Lawrence Monahan, is also part of this plan. I have been blessed to have his support, as well as the expert assistance of many talented doctors and nurses, especially the nurses on 6W at Lewis Gale Medical Center. I am sure I will be calling on all of them again as years go by.

All of my students over the years—in diverse places such as Nashville, Charlottesville, Radford, and Roanoke—have taught me to be gracious in my acceptance of constructive criticism, and they have provided feedback on my writing that was genuinely offered and gratefully received. Special thanks go to Kristi Fry, teacher of English and writing at Northside High School in Roanoke, for arranging for me to serve as writer-in-residence for Roanoke County Schools. I think it is fair to say that I learned as much or more than the students learned.

I am blessed (and lucky) to have had the love and support of all of these wonderful people. In 1961, when I was in the fourth grade at McHarg School, I had a special, sainted teacher, Marge Roberson. She knew I wanted to be a writer and she used her power, beauty, and grace to encourage me. Over the years, I would always hear from her when I had an article published. I saw her occasionally, and she would always ask about my work. She passed away in January 2011, just before I signed my contract with Penguin. I saw her for the last time at my father's funeral in 2007. She greeted me with these words: "How's my favorite writer?"

Giles Owita taught me the answer to this question. For Marge Roberson's favorite writer, every day is good.

Carol Wall
August 2013

About the Author

Carol Wall's articles and essays centering on family life have been popular features in publications such as *Southern Living* and *The Atlanta Journal-Constitution* for more than twenty years. An accomplished public speaker, Carol served as writer-in-residence for Roanoke County Schools, where high school audiences learned to look forward to her entertaining and engaging presentations. Beginning in 1973, with her first teaching job at East High School in Nashville, Tennessee—Oprah Winfrey's alma mater—Carol has been known for her ability to connect with listeners, sharing her passion for storytelling and eagerly reaching out to include even the most reluctant student. Carol and her husband have three grown children and four beautiful grandchildren. They make their home in the Shenandoah Valley of Virginia. Carol has been battling Stage IV breast cancer since 2008. *Mister Owita's Guide to Gardening* is her first book.